Books in the GREAT STARS Series
by David Thomson

Ingrid Bergman
Humphrey Bogart
Gary Cooper
Bette Davis

BETTE DAVIS

BETTE DAVIS

David Thomson

PHOTO RESEARCH BY LUCY GRAY

ff Faber and Faber, Inc.

An affiliate of Farrar, Straus and Giroux

New York

GREAT STARS

Faber and Faber, Inc.
An affiliate of Farrar, Straus and Giroux
18 West 18th Street, New York 10011

Copyright © 2009 by David Thomson
All rights reserved
Printed in the United States of America
Originally published in 2009 by Penguin Books, Great Britain
Published in the United States by Faber and Faber, Inc.
First American edition, 2010

Library of Congress Cataloging-in-Publication Data
Thomson, David, 1941–
   Bette Davis / David Thomson ; photo research by Lucy Gray. —
1st American ed.
      p.   cm.— (Great stars)
   ISBN: 978-0-86547-931-9 (pbk. : alk. paper)
   1. Davis, Bette, 1908–1989.   2. Motion picture actors and actresses—
United States—Biography.   I. Title.

PN2287.D32T46 2010
791.4302'8092—dc22
[B]

                                                          2009041760

www.fsgbooks.com

           1   3   5   7   9   10   8   6   4   2

For Grace

BETTE DAVIS

Bette Davis was twenty-three and too smart for her own good. But there she was lying on a couch at Universal in a fixed camera set-up so that any man the studio could round up came in and made movie love to her. 'You gorgeous, divine darling,' they said – they had to say something, so they had lines written for them. 'I adore you. I worship you. I must possess you.' There were fifteen of them – 'The most compulsively dedicated harlot never had a morning like mine,' she would write – and there you see how smart she was. Not just funny, but able to surmount her own indignity with caustic intelligence. She was a novice being tested for 'chemistry', or 'it', or 'sex appeal'. This was after Carl Laemmle, the head of the studio had announced – with her in the next room and the door open – 'She has as much sex appeal as Slim Summerville!' Summerville was fortyish, a country hick with a simpleton cowboy face. He was just a little niftier than his horse.

We can talk about what Bette Davis had and didn't have, and what you might like to have done to her if you were a red-blooded American male. Suffice it to say that with Bette Davis, her looks and her sexiness – her appetite for the movies – were always under question. 'Well, she was never beautiful,' you hear people say. But the same Bette Davis, in those years from 1931 to 1945 – the golden age, more or less – was nominated seven times for best actress. In the same period, Garbo got one nomination, Katharine Hepburn four, Marlene Dietrich one, Claudette Colbert three, Barbara Stanwyck three. Davis outpaced the field without ever convincing a studio – or maybe herself – that she had 'it'. Simple, unequivocal desirability. Yet something possessed her, an energy or a need that could leave every other actress seeming vacant.

The thing she asserted was that there were 'Bette Davis parts', a territory where other actresses had best not tread. For there was something fearsome in being Bette Davis, something that seemed close to consuming the woman herself. It's a part of the nature of acting in those days, and of the terrible insecurity of actresses, that several of the great parts might have been recast – Irene Dunne surely could have played Mrs Miniver, Barbara Stanwyck could have done Mildred Pierce, Katharine Hepburn could have been in *My Man Godfrey*, Claudette Colbert was actually cast as Margo Channing in *All About Eve* and I am tempted to share the lady's own imperious view, that Bette Davis would have been a natural as Scarlett O'Hara – 'It was insanity that I not be given Scarlett.' (The essence of Davis, it seems to me, is in the use of the word 'given' there, as opposed to some such construction as 'be cast as'. The 'gift' was

'Never beautiful'?

something the common people should have seen as appropriate to their queen, and it should have required no asking from her!)

In other words, competition – the helpless state of the harlot – was as open as the studio contract system allowed. And Bette Davis had at least a dozen rivals who photographed better than she did, or who had more glamour or lustre, more gender obedience and more of 'it' than she could offer. Yet she was the commanding figure of the great era of stardom and star projects. Moreover, most of that time, she was employed and held by a guys' studio where the bosses would tell her to her face that not a single man was going to pay money to see this or that project. Let's add that she had another three best actress nominations after 1945 – in *All About Eve*, *The Star* and *What Ever Happened to Baby Jane?* Come to that, one has to note and marvel how in her heady years she was not actually nominated for *Of Human Bondage*, *The Old Maid* or *The Private Lives of Elizabeth and Essex*.

I doubt there is a better example of willpower thriving in the alleged age of sex appeal. Her own insistence that she was right for a role, or the best actress around, is not always sympathetic. But it is much harder to make a case for her being wrong. She prided herself on exact judgement and insight, on reason and justice – New England virtues – and never quite realized that on the West Coast the country was run rather differently.

Ruth Elizabeth Davis was born on 5 April 1908 in
Lowell, Massachusetts. This was nine months and four
days after the marriage of her parents: Harlow Morrell
Davis, of Bates College and Harvard Law School, and
Ruth Favor, an amateur actress of some ability. The
Favors were of French descent, while the Davises had
been in Massachusetts since 1634 – and in Wales before
that. It was a Davis who had helped found the city of
Haverhill. Harlow Morrell Davis had a great dome of a
forehead, rimless spectacles and a most earnest gaze.
He would have been shocked if, say, his first child had
been delivered less than nine months after the day of
his marriage. Nevertheless, he had not intended to have
a family so swiftly and the father proved incapable of
talking to Ruth or to her younger sister, Barbara, born
eighteen months later. Aged five, apparently, Ruth
decided to alter her name to Bette – a name she had
seen on the spine of a Balzac novel. The father thought
the change was pretentious, and that attitude only
offended Bette the more. When Bette was seven, the
father left the family.

By the time Bette was twenty, she was resolved to be
an actress. The mother passed this information on to
the father, who was reported as having said, 'Let her
become a secretary! She'll earn money quicker. Bette
could never be a successful actress.' The young girl took
this as a challenge, just as she now perceived her father
as a negative force. It was a part of her larger determination to triumph, to do as she wished, and to lead what

would amount to her 'lonely life'. In 1962, Bette Davis published a short memoir called *The Lonely Life* and it is nearly shrill with her determination to take personal responsibility for everything:

I have always been driven by some distant music – a battle hymn no doubt – for I have been at war from the beginning. I rode into the field with sword gleaming and standard flying. I was going to conquer the world . . .

My father's cavalier disappearance from our home when I was a small child certainly has significance. Consider my quartette of marriages. But his hypothetical perfection as a father might have bound me to him and spoiled other men for me.

If I were making a documentary film about Bette Davis, I would cut from that observation (preferably in her piping voice – a regal, declaratory voice) into the opening scene from *The Letter*. It is night in Malaya. Clouds cross the moon. Rubber plantations are busy with their dripping business. Suddenly there is a flurry of action at one house. We hear a shot. A door opens, a man tumbles out, pursued by a small, fierce-faced woman in a long housecoat that flows as she moves. With a revolver she fires five more shots at him, and into him. It is a very arresting passage of movie and a great opening. It will be said quite soon that this woman, Leslie Crosbie, shot the man because he tried to force his attentions on her.

We don't quite believe that story. We can believe that a man might tell Leslie he loved her and even try to rape her. And she might be hurt and shocked by it. She might shoot him – once. But six shots, one after the other? In such flowing, irresistible motion. We guess that if the gun had held a dozen bullets, the man would have had to soak them all up. No, there is another story – this man has let the woman down, and she is ready, waiting, expecting such an insult, and equipped to rebuke it. And she takes no prisoners.

The Letter is one of those films for which Davis received an Academy nomination, but it is not the only one of the ten in which her character is malicious, vengeful, hostile to men, a bitch. There are similar traits in *Dangerous*, *Jezebel*, *The Little Foxes* and *Mr Skeffington*. There is more of it still – at either end of the social register – in *Of Human Bondage* and *The Private Lives of Elizabeth and Essex*. And what is Scarlett O'Hara but the ultimate bitch role in American cinema?

Now look at the faces of Bette Davis in the late '20s and early '30s. It is certainly not the case that she was not pretty. As a teenager, with long blonde hair and very friendly eyes, she was the sort of girl to draw attention wherever she went. But it was a completely natural beauty, and it had not a hint of glamour or allure. She was plainly smart, merry and quick – and her look promised sympathy and friendship, as well as teasing and mischief. It was not the look of someone consumed by a great dream of the self – like Garbo, or Joan Crawford

even. You can see, from the earliest times (and Crawford the perpetual rival was ahead of Bette Davis for years), that Davis might have dismissed Joan as a fabrication of hairdressing, cosmetics, photography and gall. Whereas Bette's was a face you might see on a beach in Maine, in summer stock, or in a shop, a face that pricked your attention. In America in the first decades of the twentieth century, Hollywood came to represent the manipulation of appearance as against an authentic, God-given naturalness. Bette Davis believed she looked like an 'ordinary' person, or an 'ordinary' genius.

Audiences might have agreed, except for the eyes. Before she arrived in Hollywood, Bette Davis had eyes that popped a little or which looked as if she might have been crying. But in real life, tears tend to make the eyes go raw, narrow and tired – and Bette's jumped open. They were startled or alert – as if she had just been touched somewhere intimate. It was thus that one saw the liquid glaze or pressure on her eyeballs and thought of tears. It was a sadness against which the pluck of her demeanour seemed all the more admirable. It is not crying, but a refusal to cry – and perhaps it leads to a determination that someone else, the man, will cry first. Decades ahead of feminism, or anything like it, Bette Davis was using stories to point up the aggressive energy of women – in an art form or a public trance justly famous for making the seductiveness of women legendary and iconic.

A fascinating comparison can be made with Katharine

Hepburn. The two women were born a year apart. They were both from old New England and respectable Protestant stock. They entered movies at around the same time. And Hepburn is the only actress of that age who – in the long run – won more nominations and Oscars than Davis. Moreover, in her public demeanour and lifestyle Hepburn was modern and a feminist as well as someone who could pierce the stupid talk of gossip magazines with her wit.

But Katharine Hepburn had a very tricky movie career so that after early success she succumbed to the idea of herself being box office poison (or outside the popular range) – and reconstructed herself in such a way that she became increasingly amenable and obedient to strong men. Thus, her Tracy Lord goes back with Cary Grant's C. K. Dexter Haven in *The Philadelphia Story* and she signals her willingness to be subordinate to Spencer Tracy in the crushing sell-out ending to *Woman of the Year*. In all her films with Tracy she yields finally (and sometimes feebly) to male 'superiority' or order. The same is true in *The African Queen*. I don't say this to attack Hepburn, or undermine her, but to define her. She altered the signals she was giving to be successful. By contrast, Bette Davis never really adapted herself. And while she knew that male audiences hardly loved her – but often liked to hate her – she did not step back from that defiance. She goes into the night and her own future fighting and giving off warning airs. The courage and the energy that required came from somewhere, and we may begin with the way a father had wronged her or walked out on her without ever explaining himself (he died of a heart attack while she was filming *Jezebel* – she was too busy to go to the funeral). Bette Davis made women's pictures, to be sure, and some are gentler or more yielding than others, but to the point of stridency in the '30s and '40s she asserted this war cry – that women do not have to take it, or be seen crying. Neither our movies nor our society have yet lived up to this intimidating example.

There's another line of thought on why Bette's father left the family: because he realized that Ruthie the mother was going to raise those girls and get at least one of them into the theatre – so get out of the way and leave her to it. The mother did everything she had to in the way of menial or common employment to support the two daughters, while claiming classical artistic poverty. They were hard up and the life was simple, and they moved around searching for the right theatrical education on the best possible terms. It's very likely that the mother was the steadiest and fiercest teacher Bette had, as well as the root of the conviction in the young woman that she would make it – no matter what.

At different times, they were in the Boston area, in New Jersey and in New York City. Bette told a story in her book that as a teenager in Boston she had posed

nude for a famous city statue – but diligent research
has never found it afterwards. Perhaps imagination
helped. At seventeen, apparently, she met the young
Henry Fonda. A kiss was exchanged and a letter pursued Fonda from the young woman assuring him that
her mother would announce their marriage very soon.
She was educated at Cushing Academy and had an early
taste for dance. Then her mother took her to audition
for Eva Le Gallienne and Bette was turned down – it
seemed to be because of a mixture of wilfulness and
frivolity. Instead she attended the John Murray Anderson Dramatic School and fell under the influence of
two very different teachers – the English actor, George
Arliss, and the new heroine of modern dance, Martha
Graham. She became convinced that movement and
gesture were vital to acting and an assertion of her
being. Davis often moves like a beast fearful of being
leashed. If she had a tail it would beat off approach.
Arliss was old-fashioned, punctilious and deep-etched.
Martha Graham was sudden, romantic and convulsive.
It does not seem a likely marriage, but keep it in mind
as you see those great passages of hysterical spontane-
ity in which Davis never for a moment seems studied.
Think of Leslie Crosbie again, firing as if each shot
had its own vital target.

By the late 1920s, Bette Davis was ready for real
work. She could look demure while behaving like an
empress; she could seem passionate and headstrong,
while she believed she was still deeply innocent. Blonde,

Eyes like pearls

with eyes like pearls too big for her head, she was very striking, but marginally pretty and certainly not beautiful. She was slender but with quite large breasts, and she could be attractively dressed in the early '30s style. But it was her edge that made her memorable – her upstart superiority, the reluctance to pretend deference to others. She was getting a reputation already, and sometimes observers felt that her confidence was somewhat ahead of the substance.

That seems to be what happened with the George Cukor Company in Rochester, New York. Cukor's company was famous for the realism of its work, and Cukor himself took on Davis and quickly asked her to understudy a key supporting performance in a play called *Broadway*. Well, the first actress was injured and Davis went on one night:

One of the six chorus girls you see from time to time in the play comes quietly down a stairway from the dressing rooms. She takes out a revolver and shoots him [the villain] . . . You don't know who she is, or why – it's a great *coup de théâtre*. Well, after the Wednesday matinee, the young girl playing this part turned her ankle and couldn't go on. I asked this blonde girl [Davis], 'Do you think you can do it?' and she said, 'Yes', and I ran her through it. She had no lines. That night I saw her performance, and she crept downstairs with her baby face and took out the revolver – and suddenly there was Bette Davis! She shot the man with an almost maniacal intensity, she *willed* him dead.

People were impressed but they noticed that Davis would not take direction. Cukor said there was nothing personal – they simply couldn't find other parts for her. It is an odd affair, and it had consequences. George Cukor (born in 1899), was one of the best film directors of Bette's time. He was also the director with a reputation for handling actresses with unique finesse. He would make ten films with Katharine Hepburn and three with Joan Crawford. But he would never direct Bette Davis. Moreover, the closest they ever came was in 1938 and the consideration over whether *Gone With the Wind* should make an alliance with Warner Brothers or with MGM. Go with Metro and you got Gable; pick Warner Brothers and you could cast Davis and Errol Flynn in the leads. The Selznick organization followed the MGM lead, but Davis may have read that as Cukor's continued veto.

So Bette moved on to the Provincetown Players and to an eventual Broadway debut in *Broken Dishes*. She also toured Ibsen's *The Wild Duck*, with Blanche Yurka. In both situations, the reviews raved while the company reported finding Bette very difficult and childishly insistent on having her own way.

Universal invited Bette Davis and her mother to Los Angeles late in 1930. She was humiliated in the routine ways and put in a picture called *The Bad Sister* but then, very quickly, she got a fair supporting role in the James Whale version of *Waterloo Bridge*, the one with Mae

Clarke in the lead. Make-up enlarged her mouth and everyone told her to use her eyes. Hedda Hopper noted that Davis 'has transformed herself into one of the town's leading ga-ga girls, picking up the personality Joan Crawford discarded when she became a lady'.

Then Warners took her up: she played a supporting part to Barbara Stanwyck in *So Big* and George Arliss asked for her in his picture *The Man Who Played God*. Arliss was English, and forty years older than Bette, but he was the first person who clearly recognized her talent – of course, he had had her as a student in New York. Warners were encouraged: she had a minor breakthrough as a sexpot in *The Cabin in the Cotton* (directed by Michael Curtiz); she was one of *Three on a Match* (with Joan Blondell and Ann Dvorak), and she was Spencer Tracy's girlfriend – before he'd met Katharine Hepburn – in *20,000 Years in Sing Sing* (which again Curtiz directed).

Bette heard that RKO planned to do a version of Somerset Maugham's novel, *Of Human Bondage*, published in 1915. As produced by Pandro Berman, the original story would be abbreviated: Philip (Leslie Howard) is an art student in Paris. When a teacher tells him he is a mediocre talent, he gives up art and determines to be a doctor – why not, he suffers from a serious club-footed condition. It is in London, living cheaply, that he meets and falls for Mildred, a waitress, a slut, a bitch, a user – a great role. And yet it was plainly the kind of affection-killing part that frightened most actresses away. That was one reason why the director John

Cromwell sent word to Bette that he knew she had the courage to do it.

So RKO approached Warners and the studio said no. Ms Davis was under contract to them and they declined to loan her out because – they said – the picture and the toxic female role would surely damage her reputation. At which point, Davis herself launched a campaign against Jack Warner personally that would last six months. At dawn and dusk, she claimed, she haunted his office with repeated pleas. And after six months Warner was so angry and vengeful that he elected to give the actress what she wanted, let that settle her.

The picture is not easy to swallow these days. But in the original novel, Philip Carey's handicap is as much lack of money and social position as a crippled foot. He is someone who runs the risk of being crushed by having ideas above his station: he is a bit like Heathcliffe. As it is, Philip is Howard at his most urbane – forty (not student age), well dressed, languid and accepting his lot. Philip really needs to be a great deal more insecure and horny – imagine the young Olivier in the part. And then there's the situation in which Philip is apparently infatuated with and constantly suckered by the iniquitous Mildred. As Bette Davis would write, 'Philip's whimpering adoration in the face of Mildred's brutal diffidence was difficult for me to believe.' Howard is too sensible, too balanced, too middle-aged, and not nearly susceptible enough to the sex that Mildred dangles.

But all of this only meant that Leslie Howard tended to sit back and let Bette dominate the picture. With palpable results. Cromwell had an odd predilection for straight-on close-ups that slow the action. And he cannot shift the basic melodramatic situation or make it more credible. But Bette is fascinating and plainly – doing her own make-up – she has mapped out a deterioration – more or less the progress in Mildred from pert, chilly waitress to the dying slut falling out of a filthy silk wrapper. Along the way, she has moments of extraordinary compelling sexuality. The zigzag walk is in evidence, her way of pushing first one shoulder forward and then the other. This is an astonishing mannerism – really no one walks like that – but Davis used it for a lifetime and it certainly draws attention to her very slim, petite figure and her full breasts. Her hair goes longer and wider – she's nearly a blonde – her eyes are rimmed in shadow and this could be Miss Depravity of 1934.

For the film to be more dramatically gripping, the script, the direction and the male lead would all need to be better. But if you grant that *Of Human Bondage* was an unusually detailed spelling out of human decline then you have an idea of how little audiences had seen yet. The death scene was apparently greeted with applause, but that bespeaks an audience that has hardly contemplated how people die. Davis says nothing in death. She is simply a collapsed or abandoned figure. This is a long way short of acting, but it is clearly the

With Leslie Howard in *Of Human Bondage*

work of an actress who had learned enough to dare a bourgeois audience to lose its sheltered sense of 'taste'. You feel the reality of a whore's life just as you do in Sickert's Camden Town paintings.

Davis received very good reviews. But when the Academy nominations appeared, only three performances were named: Claudette Colbert in *It Happened One Night* (Davis would claim that part had been offered to her, too); Grace Moore in *One Night of Love*; and Norma Shearer in *The Barretts of Wimpole Street*. In her book, Davis claimed that she was nominated, too. This is simply not true, though there was some press protest at her omission and talk of a write-in campaign whereby voters might add Davis to the ballots. In fact, the warnings from Warners proved sound: a large part of the public was horrified by the squalor of Mildred's life and the sketchy candour with which Davis conveyed it. They saw no reason to like a character not liked by her film.

There was a more practical obstacle to Davis winning. The recently formed Screen Actors Guild had gained membership at the expense of the Academy so that for the year 1934 only 95 actors remained as members of the Academy. Now, suppose that some of those 95 were Warners contract employees (heavily pressured by their studio not to vote for Davis) and one can imagine what happened. Bette herself had no doubts: she had been cheated – but rueful certainty was her nature:

My failure to receive the award created a scandal that gave me more publicity than if I had won it. Syndicated columnists spread the word 'foul' and the public stood behind me like an army. Not since that decision in 1934 was so cavalier a verdict allowed to take place. Price Waterhouse was asked to step in the next year to count the vote, which they have done ever since.

Warner Brothers were right according to their reasons. There was hardly a moment in *Of Human Bondage* when Bette was not loathsome. When she was being sweet, to be seductive, her cunning shows. Two things are shocking: the lack in an American movie woman of authentic sincerity, and the spectacle Mildred presents at the end of life – not just dissipated and reduced, but eroded and syphilitic. She is hard to look at, yet the actress concerned could take the necessary steps of make-up, or whatever – and Bette Davis was famous already for doing her own make-up.

So it's far from clear that the public 'like an army' rallied behind the cause of Bette Davis – or that she needed them. Her Oscar was not far away, no matter that when it came Bette would lead the cry that, really, Katharine Hepburn in *Alice Adams* was a far more deserving performance. We may agree, but where's the point when Oscars are more to do with passing climate than eternal justice? In the next decade, Joan Fontaine would lose for *Rebecca* and then be rewarded next year for the slighter *Suspicion*. Et cetera. There has always been the suggestion that *Dangerous* (1935) won to 'make up for' Bette's treatment over *Of Human Bondage* (1934). I suspect there's some truth in that, but I regret the sentimentality because it loses sight of how interesting a picture *Dangerous* is. Let's just say, someone was thinking when the Oscar was given to Bette Davis.

Years later, Davis tended to be dismissive of *Dangerous*: 'It was maudlin and mawkish with a pretence at quality which in scripts, as in home furnishings, is often worse than junk. But it had enough material in it to build into something if I approached it properly.' Just as the line about home furnishings smacks of Ms Davis – and shows how far above the common level of actresses she was – so the larger verdict exposes some failure to understand melodrama, or even herself.

The one-word title describes the film's central character, Joyce Heath, but why? We see her first on a New York street, fallen yet alluring, alone and hardened to it. There is that provocative walk again, and it seems fit for a gunfighter on a Western street where she knows she is so much the boss that no one dares talk to her. One man on his way to his club notices her. 'Excuse me,' he asks, 'but aren't you Joyce Heath?' Bette stares him down with insolence, and says 'No . . . You've made a mistake.' It is a great opening that pierces the heart of this self-destructive loner. She is dangerous because she cannot admit her own nature. At the very end of their marriage, Bette's fourth husband, Gary Merrill, would observe that in life she had put herself too far apart from everyone else. She said she was lonely. He thought she was alone.

Joyce Heath was an actress and a great one. Someone calls her 'a vitally tempestuous creature . . . too brilliant, too startling, a comet'. She is mentioned in the same breath as Jeanne Eagels (1894–1929), a great but tragic figure still hovering over actors as Bette Davis arrived, famous for doing *Rain* on stage and *The Letter* as a silent film. Eagels died early from booze and drugs. But Joyce Heath is in her prime still. She shows no sign of the devastation that afflicted Bette at the end of *Of Human Bondage* (which might have been modelled on the way Eagels looked in life). Joyce Heath is killing her body with gin, but her soul already bears a jinx.

Then another man sees her: Don Bellows, a fashionable young architect, about to be married to Gail Armitage. He recognizes Joyce and becomes enchanted. He sends his fiancée home so that he can talk to the actress. She is smashed on gin but when he recalls the impact of Joyce's Juliet, she picks up the scene and delivers a haunting fragment of Shakespeare – drunk but vulnerable and a mark of Davis's astonishing skill. She collapses and he takes her back to his country home to recover.

Nothing happens yet, but when Don tries to scold her back to being Joyce Heath, Davis unleashes her passion and contempt – it's a short, full speech offered with hatred: 'Pity? Pity! You dare to feel sorry for me? You with your fat little soul and your smug face . . . Why,

I've lived more in one day than you'd dare to live. Pity for me! That's very funny. Because I've never had any for men like you.'

For 1935, that line, 'your fat little soul and your smug face', is vicious and contemptuous. And it doesn't fit Franchot Tone at all, whose Don is smart, thoughtful and caring. Indeed, we know already that it was seeing Joyce Heath act that changed his life and set him on course to be an architect. She attacks him, but she is lashing herself. (It's a line that seems inspired by Bette's own venom.) She needs his rescue and we know that love is dawning. Don begins to keep two offsetting lives – town and country – with Gail in town and Joyce at his country house. He proposes to invest $80,000 of his own money in a play that will return her to the stage. But the jinx hovers, the dread that something will intervene. Joyce is so good in rehearsal that everyone anticipates success. But she is secretly married – to a hopeless wastrel who will not divorce her. So Joyce gets this man in a car and crashes it, determining to kill one or other of them.

The husband is crippled and Joyce survives. She goes on to her great success, Don marries his fiancée. And we see Joyce, a successful actress again, in the endless process of visiting her crippled husband in hospital. She has accepted responsibility for herself – the very task Bette Davis set herself in *The Lonely Life*.

The credentials on *Dangerous* do not seem promising: it was written by Laird Doyle and directed by Alfred

E. Green, yet as a film it is still alive, unexpected and complex where *Of Human Bondage* is predictable and monotonous. And Doyle is interesting: he died at the age of twenty-nine, having written five Bette Davis pictures. In other words, he knew her and may have had an interesting idea on what made her function on screen. His name does not crop up in *The Lonely Life* or other biographies. Still it's reasonable to assume a special understanding – and it's in the story and its talk that *Dangerous* is most striking and probing. (Even now, I'd love to watch Bette's eyes at the mention of 'Laird Doyle'.)

What makes the film exciting still is its grasp (not always sure) on the whole subject of whether a great actress is meant to be good on stage or happy in life. And whether these two things are possibly balanced. Quite simply, I do not know of another film of this time that understands that subject so well – unless it is Max Ophuls' *La Signora di Tutti*, made in Italy in 1934. Green and Doyle are not persuasive authors of this intricate material and Davis offers no help in suggesting that she might have urged the role into being herself. But someone at Warners had looked hard into Bette Davis and come away with a vehicle that might easily win, and deserve, an Oscar.

For the jinx is in Joyce Heath's own head and it is her failure to work out her own life. There's no doubt that the chemistry of the film was enormously assisted by the casting of Franchot Tone as Don. Tone was rich: his family owned Carborundum. He was educated at

With Franchot Tone in *Dangerous*

Cornell and he was a darling of New York theatre. He was also a very accomplished actor, with hints of strength and weakness. It's also plain that he and Bette clicked as she had not yet done with an actor. Observers noted and Bette herself admitted that she was in love with Tone – who was about to be married to Joan Crawford (this is the start of the famous rivalry between them).

I don't want to overpraise *Dangerous*, but I urge you to watch it closely: not least for the suppleness and warmth Bette shows a lot of the time – her own attraction towards the idea of sex and intimacy. There is also the terrible opposite: the need to launch into long, vituperative speeches in which her voice – so distinctive – takes on an imperial music of its own. *Dangerous* seems to know that Bette's strength is not in talk, or conversation. Sooner or later, she needs to explode over the man in her life – it is not just her strength, it is her being. It is magnificent, and it has an eloquence that no other actress of the time could match. Like that gunslinger we felt in the opening, Bette's Joyce can out-talk every man she meets. She is utterly scornful of the widespread screen convention of the time – it embraced Garbo, Joan Crawford, Margaret Sullavan, and so many others – that a woman listens to a man, and speaks briefly in response in his natural pauses. (She fills in the gaps he leaves?) Bette's screen image is always ready not just for speech, but for tirade and tumult. She storms men's feeble defences; she berates them to their knees. It is what makes her Joyce Heath – the mistress of soliloquy yet the castaway in company. And that, I suggest, is the ultimate danger foreseen by this odd picture in being a great actress, or someone as notorious as Joyce Heath.

And so Bette Davis won her first Oscar for *Dangerous*. It was presented to her by D. W. Griffith whose great ladies were always seen but not heard. At this distance, it is impossible to find any intervening hand on the picture that might have stirred in some traces of the real, perilous Bette Davis. And yet . . . In August 1932, she had made her first marriage, to Harmon Oscar Nelson, 'Ham' she called him, a band musician. She added that he was 'home, New England, stability', an amiable nonentity who seemed to stand for the lost world of her youth. They had been childhood sweethearts and now they ignored the transformation in her life by marrying in Yuma, Arizona, in 115 degrees. It would make a great scene, with the virgin fainting in the heat. Yes, she said, she was chaste until that night: 'The sweetness of first love. It still clings like ivy to the stone walls of this institution called Bette Davis.'

I know, she wrote *The Lonely Life* (from which this is quoted) decades later. But it's a kind of writing that helps explain *Dangerous*. Are you going to be surprised to hear that the marriage did not last or flourish? That is the backstory to the rapport with Franchot Tone on *Dangerous*. Bette did get pregnant. Her mother told her a child was a very bad idea at this juncture (this seems to be 1935–36). 'I understood everything intellectually. I was wretched emotionally. I did as I was told.' She had an abortion.

Warners were famous for working their contract players hard. For instance, in 1935, at $1,200 a week, Bette Davis made five pictures: *Bordertown*; *The Girl from Tenth Avenue*; *Front Page Woman*; *Special Agent*, and *Dangerous*. *Bordertown* was a Paul Muni picture, the basis of a later remake, *They Drive by Night*, in which Bette had the Ida Lupino role. *The Girl from Tenth Avenue* (from Alfred E. Green, again), is a women's picture in which Bette saves a man who then drops her – it's quite good; *Front Page Woman* is Bette and George Brent as newspaper reporters – it's flat (Brent couldn't be a daily reporter – he's a weekly columnist); *Special Agent* is Brent and Davis again in a crime story.

In that same 1935, Joan Crawford made two pictures at a far higher salary, and Katharine Hepburn made three, one of them *Mary of Scotland* – for which, incidentally, Bette had tried to get a loan-out from Warners so that she could play Elizabeth. Davis had good reason to feel she was being exploited and neglected at the same time by her studio. She won her Oscar in March 1936. Whereupon, the studio leased the use of her face for breakfast cereal ads, refused to increase her salary, and put her in *The Petrified Forest*, *The Golden Arrow* and *Satan Met a Lady*.

The first was something she could be pleased at: it was a prestige production taken from a successful

Broadway play that retained the two male leads – Leslie Howard and Humphrey Bogart (playing gangster Duke Mantee in his first breakthrough) – and in which Bette replaced Peggy Conklin. It's a rather fanciful part – the Arizona girl who wants to go to Paris and be an artist – in a man's picture, but Bette made the best of it. Whereas *The Golden Arrow* is a dud, with George Brent, and *Satan Met a Lady* is Warners' second, disastrous version of Dashiell Hammett's *The Maltese Falcon*, with Bette opposite Warren William as Sam Spade.

In career terms alone, she had reason to be depressed. Her marriage was clearly over, and it is possible that by 1936 she had had two abortions. Bette Davis thought of herself as old Yankee stock, New England, and the horror of personal failure should not be minimized. Not for the first time, she told Warners that she couldn't and wouldn't play in her next assignment, *God's Country and the Woman*, where she was supposed to be a lumberjack. (It was made finally with George Brent and Beverly Roberts and in colour, but colour is not enough.) The studio suspended her. And she quit, just like a character in one of her films – the heiress who runs away or the great actress who is in hiding.

With her mother, Bette Davis flew from Los Angeles to Vancouver, took the train across the country and then sailed on the *Duchess of Bedford* from Montreal to London. It was her intention there to join forces with Ludovic Toeplitz and make two European films outside her contract. Toeplitz had helped produce *The Private Life of*

Henry VIII and *Catherine the Great*, historical epics from the Korda Company. Now he wanted to do his own pictures, and for £40,000 (about $150,000) he had two projects for Bette: *I'll Take the Low Road*, where she would play with Douglass Montgomery, and an unnamed picture with Maurice Chevalier. As soon as they heard of this, Warners sought an injunction to stop either of the Toeplitz productions in the British courts. In life, it seemed awkward and embarrassing, but really it has all the ingredients of a great comedy. That it proved to be such a public entertainment suggests that some of the parties may have guessed that in advance.

There were no foreseeable terms under which Bette Davis could win her action. She might claim that her contract amounted to 'slavery', but it was easy for the studio to have her portrayed as a spoiled little girl, highly paid and pampered, yet still driven to the heights of vanity by her alleged fame. In fact, the theory that penalty time added on for suspensions did amount to a curtailment of freedom would have its day – the case that really secured freedom from contract servitude in Hollywood was that of Olivia de Havilland against Warners. And in 1936, Ms de Havilland had just come on board at Warners, ready to learn from the great Bette Davis.

Bette and her mother stayed in London at Claridge's and their stage was the high court in September 1936. Sir Patrick Hastings appeared for Warner Brothers and Sir William Jowitt for the actress. By this time, without money from Warners or Toeplitz, Bette was as close to broke as at any moment since she became famous. She was referred to in court as 'a very naughty young lady' – cut to a close-up of her pursed lips and baleful eyes. Yes, it plays. Bette decided to spend the whole trial staring at the judge trying to hypnotize him! There was an interval and a chance to smoke and Bette discovered that in the very next court room an American woman named Wallis Simpson was suing for divorce.

Jowitt claimed the studio contract was 'a life sentence'. Should the actress take the stand to tell tales of her misery? This point was much argued. Her lawyer 'feared that under unfriendly interrogation I would lose my temper and injure my cause'. Had he heard one of her tirades in his head? In the end, she was just a face in court, not a voice. Still, she lost the case. Warners won a three-year injunction. Davis faced bills of $50,000, which included Warners' costs. She was devastated and then George Arliss came to find her. 'Go back, my dear Bette,' he said. 'You haven't lost as much as you think. Go back gracefully and accept the decision. See what happens. I think good things. If in time you feel you're being treated unjustly, put up another fight. I admire your courage in this affair but now – go back and face them proudly.'

Was Arliss serving as an intermediary? His predictions proved true. Warners swallowed their costs. They even helped with Bette's. And thereafter they had no reason to question the courage or independence of their actress. Moreover, the case had played well with the

BETTE DAVIS   33

public. If anything, Bette had added to her popularity. She had fights to come and there were more films that she would have preferred not doing. Still, a ten-year run of key roles was about to begin in what anyone could now recognize as 'Bette Davis pictures'. But a similar lesson is apparent in most star careers: they must teach us how to watch or see themselves – and it follows from that that they may need to educate themselves.

Is it also possible that the European adventure had brought her confidence, or a feeling that she should trust her own energy? On the face of it, 1937 didn't look much better than 1936 – she had to make four pictures that were plainly Warner Brothers material: *Marked Woman* (where she plays a hooker); *Kid Galahad* (she is a fight manager's moll named Fluff); *That Certain Woman* (where she's a gangster's widow falling in love with a nice guy); and *It's Love I'm After*, which is another lost gem, like *Dangerous*.

Marked Woman appealed to Bette because it was a Warner Brothers crime picture in which the balance had been altered: the woman was the central figure here. So Eduardo Ciannelli is the big-city racketeer and Humphrey Bogart is the district attorney, supposedly based on Thomas E. Dewey. But Bette is Mary Dwight, a hostess at the Club Intimate who stands up against the mob when they bring about the death of her kid sister (Jane Bryan). Mary says she will testify against them. She is savagely beaten up, but still appears in court to finger the Ciannelli character.

For the first time at Warners, Bette was in a picture
that bore the legend 'Produced by Hal Wallis'. Wallis
had been running the show since 1933 but in the past
Bette's films had been delegated to other, very efficient
producers. Still, the shift is telling: it seems to suggest
that the studio recognized how far Bette's potential for
trouble (and quality) merited Wallis's personal attention.
And Wallis was one of the great executives in movie
history. Moreover, *Marked Woman* was directed by Lloyd
Bacon, one of the studio's front-rank directors and
someone Bette had not worked with before. The script,
too, was from bigger names – Robert Rossen (a director
in the making), Abem Finkel and Seton I. Miller. And
then Bette washed her hair.

Bette Davis, by nature, had brown hair, yet so far
in her movie career she had been a bright blonde –
somewhere between ash and bleached. Let me add this:
that in going back over Davis films of the 1930s with
friends, the most frequent remark they've offered is, 'I
never realized how lovely she was.' It's true. In film after
film – but never more than in *Kid Galahad* – Bette Davis
exudes sex appeal. The only thing that gets in its way
is her emphasis or forcefulness. But in a lot of films,
she is boyishly slim, wearing clothes beautifully – and
she took care to be very well dressed – with superb
shoulders and eyes that are like eggs beneath her sil-
very blonde look. It was an image being perfected at
Warners – with photographers Ernie Haller and Tony
Gaudio in the lead. And you have to see it to believe it.

So it's all the more striking at this point that Bette begins to go dark in her hair – less girly, less easily given to names like 'Fluff', less lightweight, more rueful and more disposed to suffering. And more certain that she must go another way than by beauty.

The process is very clear in *Kid Galahad*, the Fluff picture, if only because for nearly the last time Bette goes along with being the sweet, agreeable ingénue. She is the lover of Edward G. Robinson, a fight manager who discovers a champion in an honest kid (Wayne Morris) so that they all triumph against a wicked manager (played with startling excess by Humphrey Bogart – still plainly lost in his own villainy). Produced by Wallis, written by Seton Miller and directed by Michael Curtiz, *Kid Galahad* is an immensely entertaining picture, albeit one that's forgotten as soon as it's over. Far more than his studio colleagues, Curtiz moves the camera; he likes mirror shots; he shows a feeling for complex space that is one of the secrets of cinema. And he loves his people. There are party scenes where Bette walks around in fabulous (Orry-Kelly) dresses that barely conceal her delectable breasts, breathing one-liners that are tart, funny but kind. There's a wonderful moment when Morris's humble chump says something that appreciates the tough life a Fluff has and Bette's eyes widen at being so unexpectedly recognized. This is a woman who, at Metro or Paramount, might have been a sweetheart – she is so gorgeous. I'll say it: in 1935–37, I don't think there's a more desirable or intriguing woman in pictures than Bette Davis.

And she's getting ready to say goodbye to it.

It was while Bette Davis was in London that Margaret Mitchell's novel *Gone With the Wind* was published, and became an international best-seller. There had been some word of the book before publication and Davis believed that Jack Warner had promised her he would get an option on the novel, with her in mind. When she actually read the book Bette was even more strongly of the opinion that it was meant for her. But in the event, David Selznick bought the rights to the Mitchell book for $50,000 – not so big a sum in those days. This surely aggravated the actress's dispute with her studio, but what she did not know was that as early as 1935 Hal Wallis was looking at the play, *Jezebel*, by Owen Davis. This was far less of a piece than *Gone With the Wind*, and Bette could never quite lose her sneer at the way *Wind* had worked out. But in the event, she was lucky – just like Vivien Leigh.

The first feelings at Warners were that *Jezebel* wasn't very good. A tempestous Southern belle, Julie Marsden, loses her true love to another woman because she is wilful, unruly, self-destructive and a bitch – Jezebel. Tallulah Bankhead had been the initial casting in the play, but when she fell ill Miriam Hopkins was called up in her stead. The studio had the urge now to make Julie somehow more likeable and so the play bowed to better ideas. A group of writers were involved, one of them John Huston, and what they worked out was that in the great crisis of the yellow fever outbreak in New Orleans in the 1850s, Julie would risk her life to be with the man who had abandoned her. It was a movie about arrogance turning to self-sacrifice, and if you had had the right measuring equipment you could probably have detected Bette Davis's greedy, needy eyes pushing out a millimetre or two further.

Jezebel ended up on a far more modest scale than *Wind*: it is black and white, and it runs for only 103 minutes. It has a single dramatic situation to show the terrible overconfidence in Julie: her decision to wear a red dress to the ball, and the scandal that results in her losing the respect of Pres, or Preston Dillard (Henry Fonda). She feels sure Pres will come back to her, but when he does he has a new wife in tow, Amy (played by Margaret Lindsay, the other woman from *Dangerous*). But then the fever epidemic mounts and Julie asserts herself by nursing Pres when he falls sick. The movie ends with her escorting Pres to the island off New Orleans that awaits the dead and dying. But the wife has backed off and there is a glow of triumph mixed with mortification on Julie's selfish face.

Pres, in truth, is not much of a role and there's another male part, Buck Cantrell, assigned to George Brent. He is a long way from Rhett Butler but he has a little of that flourish, and Brent does a fair job at it – until he disappears in a duel. What shapes the film is the

Jezebel

romantic concentration on Julie, the unexpectedly sharp statements about the archaic attitudes of the South (politically *Jezebel* is a good deal more modern than *Gone With the Wind*) and the direction by William Wyler. 'He made my performance,' said Bette. 'He made the script. *Jezebel* is a fine picture. It was all Wyler. I had known all the horrors of no direction and bad direction. I now knew what a great director was and what he could mean to an actress. I will always be grateful to him for his toughness and his genius.'

What did Wyler do? Well, he kept the film tight and he never took his eye off Julie. He shaped the arc whereby her arrogance turns to contrition and he undoubtedly helped Bette place the key scenes in the overall progress of the film. And he was unafraid of the melodrama in her nature, but simply studied it as if it were a kind of madness. We never know or are asked to wonder why Julie is the way she is – similarly, Davis's best directors hardly ever question the 'taste' or good sense of her emotional energy. They ride its force. She is allowed to exist. But *Jezebel* then shows redemption setting in, and Julie's taking over of the actual role of wife is breath-taking in what it suggests: that emotional truth takes precedence over form. And so the bitch becomes a strange kind of saint; as she makes the transformation in herself she is all the more admirable and iconic. In other words, her world view is not just endorsed, but celebrated – and thus her emotional temperature becomes like the film's norm. That is why Pres's illness hardly matters; it simply leaves her in charge, reigning alone, or on his behalf. We feel after seeing *Jezebel* that everyone ought to be like Julie Marsden.

That is how things like the red dress still work in black and white – because the gesture is so much a part of Julie's vanity, or madness. Just as fever takes over the world, so Julie's passion rises to the surface. And the audience is left to believe nothing else matters. We neither know nor care who will die. Julie's gesture has settled every contest. That is why she is so serene at the end. Her story has transcended death.

Davis herself was in no doubt how much of this intensity was owed to William Wyler. She told people she was in love with the director and there was an affair between them. Wyler worked as a realist and a perfectionist, and he got Bette to drop a number of her mannerisms. He could persuade her that he was photographing a crazy kind of belief – if she believed, it should show without need of signals. And it does. The women's picture has no example of a purer self-identification than Bette's Julie, and in the last image we see of her – sailing to the island of doom – there is a perverse glory that is a first great image of isolation or loneliness.

Two other things happened during *Jezebel*: Davis's father died, and her marriage to Ham broke down. Who knows how far the liaison with Wyler had to do with that? Bette talked of marrying Wyler, yet she was afraid that his authority might take over her career entirely.

There's an odd rapport there with the relationship with Pres in *Jezebel* – for he is only really desirable when she can't have him (and after he has lapsed into silence). And it is a principle of desire in Davis the screen persona that her longing is a romantic hope that relies on being thwarted.

Jezebel opened in March 1938, by which time *Gone With the Wind* had hardly advanced in a little less than two years. Some reckoned that Julie Marsden was a full-scale screen test for Scarlett O'Hara, but David O. Selznick was highly irritated at the way Warners had stolen a march on his project and may have lost interest in Davis because of it. In the early summer of 1938, Selznick was still considering two master plans for making *Gone With the Wind*; one included MGM: they would deliver Clark Gable and $1.25 million in funds, in return for which Loews the parent company would distribute the film. Or Warner Brothers would package Errol Flynn and Bette Davis and offer $2.1 million in funds. Selznick was in turmoil over which way to go – though Davis would later declare that she couldn't imagine Flynn playing Rhett.

We know how it turned out, yet we're left to wonder how good – and how unique – Bette Davis might have been as Scarlett. She could have carried it off, and she might have been splendid in banter with Gable (they would never play together). Leigh – five years younger and far less known – had the benefit of novelty and I think she gives an impression of turbulent youth that was already beyond Bette's reach. There is this problem, too: that Bette was established as the bitch, while Vivien Leigh was fresh ground for the audience. She could find the bitch and the romantic in Scarlett and the audience felt that they were sharing in the discovery. Scarlett deserved immense newness. Whereas Bette Davis was already an atmosphere that cast a shadow on her parts. Imagine the great length of the Selznick film without Vivien Leigh's volatility or unpredictability.

Davis won her second Oscar for *Jezebel*, and by the time it was awarded *Gone With The Wind* was being shot – though its first director, George Cukor, had given way to Victor Fleming. For a moment, it looked as if the Southern belle contest had been settled. The other nominees for 1938 were Wendy Hiller as Eliza in *Pygmalion*, Fay Bainter in *White Banners* (a film that has slipped away), Margaret Sullavan in *Three Comrades* and Norma Shearer in *Marie Antoinette* (a courtesy nod to the celebrated widow). It can't have been too much of a contest – for that you have to look ahead a year when Leigh's Scarlett beat Garbo in *Ninotchka*, Greer Garson in *Goodbye, Mr Chips*, Irene Dunne in *Love Affair* and the beginning to be ubiquitous Bette Davis in *Dark Victory*.

So much for 1939? Well no, not quite. *Jezebel* was released on 10 March 1938 and from then until the end of 1939 Ms Bette Davis (so lately mistreated by her own studio and denied rewarding parts) opened in another five films. They are *The Sisters* (14 October

1938); *Dark Victory* (22 April 1939); *Juarez* (10 June 1939); *The Old Maid* (2 September 1939); *The Private Lives of Elizabeth and Essex* (11 November 1939). Every one of them is vital in what we mean by 'Bette Davis', yet arguably only one of them, *Dark Victory*, is secure in, say, the top five she ever made. This is a measure of the extraordinary range and dynamic she had achieved in a matter of a few years, and the resolve of her studio to find material for her.

The Sisters is the least known of the five, and it is a film that reveals several confusions: as it is billed, it is a picture with 'Errol Flynn and Bette Davis', yet as it plays it is a Davis vehicle. Why that title? Well, Bette plays Louise, the eldest of three sisters in Silver Bow, Montana. The other two are Anita Louise and Jane Bryan, and at the outset the younger two are cheery, competitive and modestly sisterly while Louise is clearly detached – older, calmer, wiser, more intelligent and possibly even an example of the 'new woman'. A San Franciscan newspaperman, Frank (Flynn), is passing through town. He mutters vaguely about social changes: the mood that will elect Teddy Roosevelt, and he even mentions what Dreiser is doing with the novel (*Sister Carrie* had appeared in 1900). Frank talks of writing a novel himself. He asks for her help, and she is eager to be a part of it. Alas, the film denies us that interaction because almost inevitably it would lead to a critique of the society in which they exist. And in 1938 – whatever the state of the world – Hollywood was anxious to assist in maintaining the status quo.

But this opening promises a good deal: Louise is clearly made for more than Silver Bow; Frank is just as plainly a charming, impulsive wastrel. She falls for him. Davis said she never liked or admired Flynn, yet briefly there is a chemistry between them, that of the orderly woman knocked off her feet by an unworthy man. It is intriguing and we just about believe in their sudden elopement.

As Frank will put it, their marriage makes her stronger and him weaker. There is talk of him writing a novel, but it might be far more interesting if Louise grew into being the author. Instead, she becomes secretary to the owner of a department store. Frank sinks ever lower and he elects to go off to the China Seas the day before the San Francisco earthquake (some wastrels are born lucky). There is a fairly frightening evocation of that big day as a room collapses on Bette Davis. Of course, she survives. Frank comes back, just as Louise is reckoning to marry her boss. But instead of being the independent woman who has learned enough to take care of herself she collapses in the weakling's arms again and then, at an electoral dance that repeats the opening of the film, just as Taft is being elected, so the three sisters stand together in a ridiculous pose offering us the title of the film and the notion that their togetherness is like a flag for America. It's sisterhood as a lowest emotional denominator, and it's a film in which Bette Davis has to accept her character's necessary bowing to the male order.

But in the first half hour it's a new Davis: quiet, thoughtful, alone in the world and all the more intriguing because of her weakness for Frank. Flynn, apparently, got little help from Davis, but he is very good. As directed by Anatole Litvak, the film cannot escape being a mess, with cutaway scenes to keep us posted on the other two sisters' lives in the broadest way. So it comes down to being an antique women's film, with the wife settling for the wastrel again instead of exercising any intelligence or independence. And it has to be said that Bette Davis plays the few obligatory scenes of self-pity with zeal, or relish. Still, in her mind, the actress was ready and eager for parts that made her heroines free at last — it was just that, too often, that freedom was won at the cost of madness, murder, death or their blurring amalgam, hysteria. *The Sisters* is a bad film, but sometimes the bad films show the diseases in Hollywood more clearly than the robust ones.

But was Davis herself clear about the issue? Or was she one more confused woman? Litvak apparently shot another ending, where Louise abandoned Frank and settled with the store owner. But the audience didn't warm to such practicality. Commenting later, Davis said, 'This is not at all a happy ending because it would be out of character for Frank to become a steadfast husband. That would be as foolish as thinking Errol Flynn would make a long-time husband. Who would be so foolish? Well, Louise, would, of course. Louise is a romantic and believes, or at least hopes, it will be permanent. It was a very Bette Davis thing to do. Romantic foolishness is almost certainly doomed . . . My character

was a romantic fool like me.' Stardom's last power
occurs when the actress believes it has consumed her.

A very striking underground principle begins to
emerge: that men in movies can be criminal, violent,
hostile and flagrantly anti-social – but the process must
kill them. And women may come to the brink of their
intelligent senses (an equivalent danger) – so long as
'romantic foolishness', madness or death rescues them
in time. Warner Brothers knew this principle as far as
actors were concerned: it was the secret to Cagney and
all the other studio toughs. But as the screenwriter
Casey Robinson observed, in 1938, Warners really didn't
have much experience with women's pictures.

Robinson had written *It's Love I'm After*, and emerged
with the conviction that Bette Davis 'was a great, great
untapped talent'. Far from an ideal ingénue, Davis
struck Robinson as a looming star in a genre Warners
were almost unaware of. Consciously or not, he became
determined to find her suitable material, and he fell
upon an old love – the play, *Dark Victory*. This had been
a Broadway flop (by George Brewer and Bertram Bloch)
in 1934, with Tallulah Bankhead playing the heiress who
discovers she has a fatal brain tumour. Others had
planned to do it as a movie: David Selznick dreamed of
filming it with Garbo, and then Carole Lombard. But
once he'd seen *It's Love I'm After*, Robinson believed in it
as nothing but a Davis vehicle. Jack Warner was strongly
against the venture, and Selznick had to lose interest
first. But Robinson persevered, with Hal Wallis's sup-

port, and with Edmund Goulding directing it was resolved that Davis would play Judith Traherne.

To this day, there are still very few pictures about a person's encounter with death and one can see Jack Warner's alarm, that *Dark Victory* was really about nothing except death – even if you threw in the extra that Judith will fall in love with her doctor, Dr Steele (George Brent), and marry him. There's a clue there, I fear: for marrying one's doctor is a marked concession to fantasy, and so much less challenging than the belated attempt to find a purpose in life. Judith Traherne is a rich young woman, living on Long Island. She's not a nitwit (as the film says at one point), but she is doing nothing with herself, except raising horses and having giddy spells. As it is, she already has fatal symptoms as the film opens. It is not that she discovers the proximity of death. It is there from the start, and it leaves her no room to play a useful life. I am not necessarily calling for some drastic act of self-discovery or do-gooding. I mean simply an intellectual process that might find something worth living for as death draws nearer. And a very solicitous doctor, played with true gentleness by Brent, is not answer enough, despite the terrific drama of their first encounter.

Steele questions her, and we know he has guessed her illness. He chides her for putting herself above doctors, whereupon Bette has a classic Davis speech, the tirade as view of life: 'I've never taken orders from anyone and as long as I live I shall never take orders – from anyone. And here's something else. I'm well, absolutely well! I'm young and strong and nothing can touch me. Neither you nor Dr Parsons can make an invalid out of me. And now I'm going.'

To which Steele replies. 'That's right! Run away because you're frightened.' She whirls, and the move is like a fragment of dance, as well as instinctive Davis. But then Brent's calm diagnosis tells her what is what – they made a lot of films together and this is their best scene, with his dry manner challenging her temper.

What's left, therefore, is nothing but the opportunity for Bette Davis to go 'crazy' (or become more herself) as death draws nearer. The film is a classic. It was a great hit, and it was important in that it was her first smash hit – and in what seemed like a very daring role. Alas, the film does not stand up too well. It caves in to the notion that all a woman ought to want or need is romantic happiness or glorious demise, and all that really signifies diminishment of faculties is a mounting shrillness or hysteria. So Bette never loses her looks, her charm or her histrionic energy. Nothing remotely like the shadow of ordinary illness overtakes her. She just climbs into bed at the right moment, accompanied by Max Steiner's soaring music. It's not the worst way for spoiled babies to die.

It's clear that fans of Davis and the school of imper-sonation were ready to see death as the ultimate challenge. But Judith Traherne is not very interesting, and easily drawn to the twin poles of defiant pluck and bad luck.

But this was Davis's favourite picture, and the one she felt most fulfilled by. That self-belief is not to be taken lightly. It refers back to the kind of romantic foolishness Davis esteemed, and it helps us realize the limits to what she meant by big or worthy parts. It is possible to imagine Judith Traherne played with increasing quietness, with that hidden intelligence that marks Louise at the start of *The Sisters*. And that's a fascinating project. Then, if the doctor falls in love with her, perhaps a wiser Judith could see that he has been carried away by melodrama and gesture. They can be friends instead, and she can do something – in just the way the doctor wants to study cells to see how cancers occur. Being in love in a movie ought to signal growth and change, and so death should bring some advancement. Yet Judith stays defiantly herself. That passed once for courage and flamboyant acting. But now it shows the prison of the women's picture.

Juarez is a study in another kind of imprisonment. Yet in 1938–39, it must have seemed to Warners like an important movie. Of course, it is the kind of history picture about people who never met in reality. But with a European war within sight, there were good reasons for America to broadcast its brotherhood with Mexico. So in this strange account of the times of the Emperor Maximilian and Benito Juarez the film takes every opportunity to stress the sympathy between Juarez and Lincoln. Indeed, one of the scriptwriters, John Huston, had worked out a very tidy apologia for the project:

'Aeneas MacKenzie, Wolfgang Reinhardt and I worked in complete harmony. Wolfgang had a scholar's knowledge of Europe during the period of Napoleon III and the Habsburgs; I was a Jeffersonian Democrat espousing ideals similiar to those of Benito Juarez; and MacKenzie believed in the monarchical system.'

They worked for a year and were happy with their script, but then Paul Muni – the appointed Juarez – enforced his right to reappraise and rewrite the project (if it was to have the privilege of his presence). Muni and his wife required more Juarez, or more Muni, and since the actor had conceived of a statuesque presence – bronze, impassive and burdened with self-importance – the drama became longer, slower and less compelling.

A fatuous but vicious Louis Napoleon (Claude Rains, without much guidance or restraint) sends the feeble Maximilian to be monarch of Mexico while the United States is distracted by Civil War. He is played by Brian Aherne as a little boy who talks to his teddy bears and who wants benign peace in the playroom. But he has a wife – Carlotta as she is called in the film (Bette Davis). In fact, 'Charlotte' was Belgian, yet Davis plays the part in raven black hair and staring gypsy eyes – as if to suggest an emotional affinity with Mexico, or the likelihood that her character will go mad. So it proves. Carlotta goes back to Paris and has one great scene where she subjects Napoleon to a Bette Davis tongue-lashing. But once that is over she faints and settles into dementia – she lived another sixty years, but only in fact. In Mexico,

Maximilian is lost – he has his own date with Manet's firing squad.

Davis and Aherne were as put off by Muni's tyranny as was Huston. William Dieterle directed, and he was Muni's trusted craftsman. Carlotta is an appendage: she and Maximilian are said to be deeply in love, yet they seem incapable of having a child together. The best to be said is that the picture is some kind of tribute to Mexico and its patient heroes – not just Juarez, but a fiery Porfirio Díaz (played by the young John Garfield). Alas, the picture only shows how trashy and stilted American–Mexican relations have always been in movies. If there is accuracy in this portrait of Maximilian, he was a very strange figure in history. If there is a meaning for 1939 in the allegory of democracy, it is so vague as to escape register. In short, it feels like an unfortunate prestige production in which someone has prevailed upon Bette Davis to 'do' Carlotta, without realizing that her strength and intelligence are the only fit rivals for Juarez's granite self-regard.

Graham Greene, who knew Mexico already, professed himself impressed by both Muni and Aherne. He says he smelled the Aztec and the Habsburg. I can only wish that the film had more scenes like the row between Napoleon and Carlotta: there, for a moment, the posed portraits spring to life. So, if you are Mexican, it is a very stirring story; and if you are a Habsburg, it is all too sad to contemplate. But the world wants more, and can't help noticing that Bette Davis has all

With Howard Hughes

the equipment to play a great romantic tyrant in a costumed epic — if the history department at Warners could think of anyone.

Still, Bette Davis got top billing in *Juarez*, and imperial madness could be regarded as a fine wine. It was at just this moment that Davis took the key step of taking on Jules Stein and MCA as her agency. That was a pioneering step at a moment when MCA were new to Hollywood and movies, and it improved her contract to $4,000 a week. Moreover, it was also evident that the rampaging sensualist in Bette was getting around. There had been the affair with Wyler (which apparently came close enough to marriage to remind Bette that he was Jewish). There was a serious romance with George Brent around the time of *Dark Victory*. And there was her affair with Howard Hughes, something that led Bette to be unusually outspoken:

By that time, I was married to Ham only in name. We were usually separated because of his work or my work, or both. When we were together, there was nothing left between us. Any happy days we had had were in our memories almost entirely before we married. The terrible distance when we were together was harder to bear than when we were apart. We no longer communicated with each other at all. And our sex life had disappeared, a woman who's been with just one man for a long time is practically a virgin again . . .

You know, I was the only one who ever brought Howard

Hughes to a sexual climax, or so he said at the time. No, of course you don't know. It's true. That is to say, it's true that he said it. Or, let's say, I believed it when he told me that. I was wildly naive at the time. It may have been his regular seduction gambit. Anyway, it worked with me, and it was cheaper than buying gifts. But Howard Huge, he was not.

I liked sex in a way that was considered unbecoming for a woman in my time. The way I felt was only considered appropriate for a man, it was both a physical and emotional need. Of course, it had advantages in the pleasures it brought me. No question about that. But it also made me a victim.

This rare struggle – between abandon and control – takes us straight back to the character she played in *Dangerous* in such a way that we can see how sex and acting are mutually interchangeable elements. The woman wants to be a true bearer of passion, but she is an actress at her best as women nearly out of control. She would be with a man – if she wasn't working so often. And what is the force that draws her on? That of a woman half-crazy for a man, for rapture or ecstasy, but terrified it will leave her a victim. It's touching that Davis is at the same time so candid and yet so aware of how naive she was. No wonder she found the Joan Crawfords cynical and even meretricious. No wonder at this point in her life she was tempted to play the Virgin Queen, Elizabeth I, at sixty.

The marriage to Ham was ending, in acrimony and farce. The poor man tried to tape-record Bette's coupling with Howard Hughes. He was far less wealthy than she was, and there was talk in the settlement that Bette had to persuade Warners to advance the ex-husband some pocket money. But she was devastated, too. There was enough of the New England girl in her longing for her marriage to be perfect. And she was at the same time smart and impulsive enough to find it very difficult to plan or adhere to a cool line of behaviour. Her problem with men surely shows on screen. In *Dark Victory*, there had been not a glimmer of sexual chemistry with Humphrey Bogart or Ronald Reagan. But she was turned on by the upholstered suaveness of George Brent. He was like Franchot Tone or Leslie Howard, and a signal that Bette hardly worked well with powerful or macho male stars. Yes, she could protest that she was at a man's studio, where the standard line-up was hardly calculated to work well with her.

In hindsight, you may say, Well, surely she could have played Lily opposite Barrymore in *Twentieth Century*, or Hildy with Cary Grant in *His Girl Friday*. Is it a problem of being unsuited to comedy? In the quarrel scene in *Juarez* with Claude Rains, the audience is longing for Rains to respond in kind – we want to see those two at each other's throats. But in love or grief or warfare, there was already the suggestion that Bette's enormous energy and flaring eyes would rise to a pitch where men felt insecure. It's true that George Brent finally made eleven films with Davis and usually found a way to be the glove that fit her trembling hand (or fist). Davis herself loved playing with Claude Rains (they worked together four times). But apart from those two, Bette never had anything like a regular partner – and eventually that made for the assumption that she was in a world of her own.

The dilemma of the women's picture, and its tricky interaction with an actress's own life, is glaringly apparent in Davis's next film, *The Old Maid*. In many reference guides, this picture is recommended: Leonard Maltin gives it three and a half stars and calls it 'soap opera par excellence'. I think it is dreadful and odious, but the reasons for those differences are not just entertaining. They may lead us deeper into the odd framing of Davis's own mind.

In advance, *The Old Maid* seems promising. It comes from a Zoe Akins play, itself adapted from Edith Wharton's novel of 1924. The play was produced on Broadway in 1935 (with Helen Menken and Judith Anderson in the lead roles), and when it won the Pulitzer prize there was such dismay that the New York Drama Critics introduced their own awards. Paramount owned the rights first, and Virginia Van Upp (later of *Gilda*) did a screenplay. But then the project was picked up by Warners. The movie is produced by Hal Wallis and Henry Blanke (with Jack Warner in personal attendance). Edmund Goulding would direct, and the screenplay is by Casey Robinson – thus it's the team that did *Dark Victory*, all anxious to repeat their own success.

Robinson found the play too saccharine, so he

planned a modification: 'That element was hatred. I believed that putting salt into the sweet would make it a more rounded vehicle altogether and certainly more suitable for Ms Davis. We purchased the vehicle, and I went to work. Now, hate is like love; you don't portray hate by having a scene in which you say "I hate you" unless all other devices fail. And a scene in which you say "I love you" is a very bad love scene. It had to be in the whole atmosphere of the piece. It must underline everything. It must be between the lines.'

At which point, I think it is best to tell the story of the film. It is 1861, the Civil War is beginning. In a large, well-to-do house, one sister, Delia (Miriam Hopkins), is about to be married to Jim Rawlston (James Stephenson). Her sister and chief bridesmaid, Charlotte (Bette Davis), says she doesn't know whether to laugh or cry, and she is plainly anxious to be married herself. A telegram comes announcing the arrival of Clem Portis (George Brent), an old beau of Delia's, still under the impression that he will marry Delia. Charlotte heads Clem off – and we can see that she likes him, too. But he insists on being rejected by Delia, and so Charlotte tries to comfort him.

The years of the war pass. We see Clem's grave (he died at Vicksburg – alas, no more George Brent). Delia is married with children. And Charlotte, somehow, is running a home for about twenty foundlings. She is very fond of one of them, Tina (unfortunately one of the least amiable children in American film – quite an intense competition). But Charlotte, it seems, is on the point of marrying Joe Rawlston (Jerome Cowan). Then Delia works out the truth – Charlotte was said to be 'ill'. She went west for her health. And when she returned she was 'with' Tina. (How no one noticed this at the time is a mystery for all of us.) Delia is stricken in the core of her stupid respectability, but she is jealous, too, that Charlotte got that far with Clem. So she stops the marriage to Joe by alleging that Charlotte is likely to develop 'lung fever' and therefore should not marry. She also 'adopts' or steals Tina, leaving her sister in the sad position of Aunt Charlotte, the old maid.

This gets us to about the 45-minute mark in a film that will last 95 minutes. In the second half, Tina grows up to be Jane Bryan, and Bette Davis goes through a gray talcum powder make-over so that everything that once shone is now lacklustre to match the life she leads – that of increasing alienation from the Tina who favours Delia and regards Charlotte as a frigid, lifeless shrew. Charlotte has only one form of response: Bette Davis can and does indicate in every glance and gesture that she is a far subtler actress than Miriam Hopkins. The story goes that on the set Hopkins sought to upstage Davis by underplaying. It is no contest – but only in such a way that Davis's icy, perverse skill supports and sustains the absurd masochistic insistence of her character. Hers is suffering for its own sake in a situation where only the idiocy of the characters (the Rawlston brothers are nincompoops) and the overall reluctance of people to talk about the truth allows the tortured situation to persist.

Casey Robinson would later blame Goulding for not controlling the players better. But Robinson might have paid more attention to the defects of a script in which huge events occur after a fade-out but very little actually happens on screen. One conclusion emerges: that Davis's own resolve is to ignore the faults of the script and to insist on the gruesome, silent ordeal of Charlotte. The self-pity is as large as the creeping malice, and as unpleasant, but *The Old Maid* supports a world in which people would sooner suffer in silence than use talk to clear up a situation and advance their own lives. Indeed, it is hard to think of a picture that so fully enacts and sustains the wretched prison of the women's picture genre. Bette Davis is by far the strongest force in the movie, and she deserves not just the blame but the understanding for how the picture works out. To watch it now in silence is to put a serious strain on feminist sensibilities. In turn, that is a way of recognizing how far Bette Davis – clearly in comparison with other actresses like Hepburn, Crawford, Dunne – welcomed the melodramatic pressure and its ultimate destiny – madness. The reluctance to pursue health and maturity is the most marked thing about the picture – and, oddly, the only reason now for watching it. We have to go to the very shrewd Molly Haskell to pin down the double-thinking over the 'lost' child. 'The child that is seen as a means of shoring up a marriage becomes the wedge that drives a couple apart. But to admit this, to admit any reservations about having children or toward the children themselves is to commit heresy. The only way to express this hostility is through a noble inversion: the act of sacrifice, of giving them up. Thus, the surrender of the children for their welfare is a manoeuvre for circumventing the sacred taboo, for getting rid of the children in the guise of advancing their welfare.'

What did this mean to Davis? She observed that she felt gratified at the end of the picture sitting in a crowded theatre and hearing audiences cry. That is a revelation and an indictment of her taste, as much as of her own dreams. And I think it ran in the family. Davis had this to say about the influence of her own mother:

'There was nothing wishy-washy about Ruthie. Even her defects were monumental. She could be brutally honest, yet self-deceptive about the most trivial thing. She was the wisest person I ever knew, while at the same time, the most childlike.' It's uncanny how well that description fits the feeling we get from many Bette Davis films.

I'm not sure that any level of familiarity or observation can ever untangle everything an actress is deriving from and giving to a role. But there's no point in studying a career without recognizing the problem. Actresses must believe in their parts first, if we are to be moved in our turn. When she made *The Old Maid*, Davis had not yet had children, nor found much joy in marriage. I think it's reasonable to argue that the film reflects some melodramatic finality in those areas – and more than that, a kind of lonely triumph. By contrast – and looking just at 1939–40 – there is a warmth, an intelligence, fun and a readiness for life in Katharine Hepburn (*The Philadelphia Story*), Irene Dunne (*Love Affair*) and Margaret Sullavan (*The Shop Around the Corner*) that are admirable. By contrast, the actress who plays the older Charlotte in *The Old Maid* – smothered in the ashen look of mortification – is advertising herself, her fineness and her necessary isolation.

So imagine a story that might go something like this: a rich woman, the head of companies and estates, believes she has fallen in love with one of her young executives. She sends this man on an overseas mission, as a test of his ability. But in his absence, others in the company whisper to the woman about her lover's dishonesty. She is torn over what to believe. She charges the young man with treachery. He denies the charges and says he loves her. But she cannot trust her deeper feelings. She says she will dismiss the young man and never see him again. She expects him to beg for mercy and acknowledge her power. But the young man is too proud. He says she must trust his love – or not. So she dismisses him. Except that, she goes a little farther than that. She has his head chopped off. This woman is not just head of the company and its estates. She is Queen Elizabeth I of England (Bette Davis) and he is Robert Devereux, the Earl of Essex (Errol Flynn).

Maxwell Anderson had opened his play, *Elizabeth the*

Queen, in 1930, with Lynn Fontanne as Elizabeth and
Alfred Lunt as Essex. It was a role Davis had dreamed
of and she was ecstatic when Hal Wallis bought the
property for her. She took pleasure in surrendering her
hair and eyebrows for the part. Alas, Errol Flynn was
'the only fly in the ointment'. Davis had set her heart on
Laurence Olivier, who had just finished shooting *Wuther-
ing Heights*. 'He was arrogant, beautiful, virile and
talented,' Davis would write. 'In all scenes I dreamed he
was playing Essex.' In every movie dream, the un-
possessed field is greenest.

Bette was thirty, and in the script Elizabeth was sixty.
Yet the actress was only struck by the resemblance
between herself and a Hans Holbein portrait that she
was studying. And since the film was to be done in
colour – her first – Davis took immense pains over the
Queen's ginger hair and high white skin tones. More
than that, she told costumier Orry-Kelly to make the
clothes authentic Tudor, no matter that the costume
shop had planned to lighten up on the layers of under-
wear and the heavy fabrics to spare Bette in the heat of
the Technicolor lights.

Despite that preparation, Warners insisted on regard-
ing the picture as just another project. Fearful that too
few in the audience would know who Elizabeth or
Essex might be, the studio was going with the title 'The
Knight and the Lady'. Bette had a fit. She said she would
back out unless it was at least 'The Lady and the Knight',
and she added that if the public could be trusted to

know who 'Juarez' was then surely 'Elizabeth and Essex' was safe. Today, there's an Elizabeth in so many actresses' portfolios, and hicks in Duluth can be expected to know whether Walsingham was left-handed, but in 1939, War- ners' timidity opted finally for *The Private Lives of Eliza- beth and Essex*, harking back to Alexander Korda's success with *The Private Life of Henry VIII*. Maybe 'He Loved the Boss' was what they should have gone for.

The picture was nominated for five Oscars – in craft areas that included the art direction, the colour photog- raphy and the sound – but in fact Warners reported a suspicion in the public that this might be a British film! Norman Reilly Raine and Aeneas Mackenzie had done the script and it turned out a fair compromise between swashbuckling (Flynn putting down rebellion in Ire- land) and feminist gloom (the Queen sinking into ever greater loneliness). The Hollywood lesson was that a queen with some appetite for an emotional life was bet- ter off following Marlene Dietrich's Catherine the Great in *The Scarlet Empress* (choose your bodyguards so they know what a body needs) than imitating the harrowed close-ups of an ageing virgin.

It may have been in Davis's mind that no one else could have played Elizabeth – though Flora Robson had done it in the English film, *Fire Over England*, and Katharine Hepburn had had her shot at Mary Queen of Scots for John Ford. In the same way, who else had died on screen from a cancer? Who else had turned a pretty young woman into cold stone the way Davis had

in *The Old Maid*? Bette Davis had done just about everything except have a good time and let the fun show.
Some saw her as a bitch. She may have preferred the
word 'tragedienne'. Others placed Davis as a flame of
persistent, if not dedicated, unhappiness. The most
interesting aspect of the debate was the degree to which
her on-screen frustrations were now working in harmony with her real-life failure. For years, Davis had
proudly proclaimed that a woman could have it all –
artistic glory and private happiness. But wasn't it really
the case that the public had already learned to mistrust
her smile, or see it as a harbinger of distress?

Bette Davis had just completed an intense period of
work. She was enormously successful, and esteemed.
She was without doubt the leading movie actress of the
day. She needed rest, and so she thought of her old
New England. Yes, it happened, but that's no reason
not to see it as a scenario that might have appealed to
Warner Brothers and to Bette herself.

So imagine this great star – call her Bette Davis –
exhausted and at the end of her tether. She needs to
replenish her energy; she wants to regain her roots. And
so she retreats, for a while, to New Hampshire and
Vermont. In the film, whatever the truth in life, we are
going to place her arrival in fall foliage season – the
colours in nature speak to her emotional upheaval.

Now, Bette has known Hollywood men, some of them
world-famous, and she has tired of the way they speak of
love when they mean self-love. But then, one day in a

quiet country hotel in New Hampshire she meets a new kind of man. His name is Arthur Farnsworth. He is handsome, urbane and he is from an old New England family. Or so it seems. He stirs Bette in ways she cannot explain: 'Farney' is the real thing, and a salutary corrective after all the mirror-gazers in Hollywood. You see, Bette doesn't really approve of that place in southern California. On an impulse she buys land and a house nearby. She becomes closer with Mr Farnsworth, without ever quite knowing him. He has mysterious contacts. He can fly, and he often goes away on missions. Bette sometimes wonders in a playful way whether he is a secret agent. She is too spellbound to push her questions. The attraction builds, but uncertainty lingers. There are calls from Warners to return. Bette is in two minds. Farnsworth could be Cary Grant. He loves her – she thinks – yet he's curiously uninterested in her big life. Sometimes she has to remind him that she's a star.

They marry (this is in December 1940), but she doesn't ever know that much about him. Bette begins to be bored with him. She is back at work again, of course, absorbed in new films and sometimes flirting with her directors. Farney comes and goes. And then on 23 August 1943, while walking on Hollywood Boulevard, he cries out and collapses. No one is quite sure whether Bette is there at the time or not. Two days later, he is dead. There is an investigation, of course, and it emerges that perhaps Farney suffered a head injury some time before, one that took time to develop . . . Are you believing this? Because it really happened. And has never been explained. There were some who wondered if Bette had been involved. On one occasion, she admitted pushing him earlier on the fatal day so that he had a fall. This occurs on the eve of the making of *Mr Skeffington*. The start is delayed a week for the funeral and the inquiry. And then Bette goes back to work in a haze of guilt and confusion. She remembers that they had quarrelled just before the bad day on Hollywood Boulevard. But she can't get over the strange way in which this New England gentleman should end up dying on that flagrant street.

So that is the second failed marriage. You can see how readily friends must be telling her, 'Marry an actor. They're easier.' Equally, don't rule out the possibility that Arthur Farnsworth, strolling on Hollywood Boulevard, had just come out of a screening of *All This, and Heaven Too*, and fell as he asked himself what this dictatorial New England girl who kept saying she wanted to get away from garbage was doing when she made such prim, sententious claptrap in a mood that suggested she thinks she is doing Proust. Maybe Arthur's head just goes into an impossible swim at the memory of one more close-up where his wife raises her eyelashes to show pooled tears like exhausted seamen raising sail in a stupefied Pacific. How much of this do I have to see, he may ask himself, without losing any chance of being a man of mysterious distinction. He has tried. But now he sees that his wife is nothing but a trashpot.

There really is such a movie, called *All This, and Heaven Too*. It begins in America around the middle of the nineteenth century. A young French woman arrives to teach at an academy for young ladies. She is demure, she is by Jane Eyre out of Emma Bovary, *le beurre* it would not melt in *sa bouche*. But those nasty American girls are on to their new teacher. They know she is the figure in an immense foreign scandal, and they exhibit their open American spirit with crushing reminders of it. So, what does the teacher do? She goes into an enormous flashback to tell her story.

Her name is Henriette Deluzy-Desportes. Once upon a time in la France she took a job as governess to the duc and duchesse de Praslin. He (Charles Boyer) was a sweet man, amiable and generous, but stricken by the savage harshness of his wife (Barbara O'Neil). The duchesse becomes jealous of Henriette – *pourquois pas*? For the governess and her husband are inclined to get into quite intense interlocking close-ups and sympathies where the dewy moisture of romance shows in their eyes. Of course, *les enfants* adore their 'mademoiselle', because she teaches them affection and fun along with grammar and table manners. The duchesse dismisses Henriette and then denies her a letter of recommendation. The Praslins argue and fight. Next morning the duchesse is dead. The duc is arrested and the governess is regarded as an accomplice. The duc takes poison and dies, but not before close-ups and understandings swim together. Henriette goes free –

there is no evidence against her. But will the scandal ever be removed?

Will it? Her American girls mob her at the end of the story and there is every indication that Henriette will be acclaimed as director of lacrosse and love affairs at the school!

This was the latest work from that group of men who 'understood' Bette Davis: it was a Hal Wallis production, with David Lewis in attendance. Casey Robinson wrote the script – in confectioner's custard – and Anatole Litvak directed. *All This, and Heaven Too* (which might be read as a religious title, I suppose), was a film that lasted 143 minutes. It was nominated for Best Picture in a group that included *Rebecca*, *The Letter*, *The Grapes of Wrath*, *The Great Dictator* and *The Philadelphia Story*. It is insufferable. Even Ms Davis allows that the script had problems, though she insists that she found Boyer a delight to work with.

And then, back-to-back, a film that bears witness to the failures of the Hollywood system, and one that leaves one wishing for its best days to return. The very vague heaven in which Henriette and her duc might be reunited gives way to the Malayan sky at night, where the moon fights with clouds chased by Max Steiner's ominous music. Already we are in the Southeast Asia of the mind where rubber trees ooze and native workers do their best to sleep in the heat. No, the film has not left Burbank, but the melodrama now is in sure hands so that the film that follows is not simply far more compelling than *All This, and Heaven Too*. It says quite a lot about the lives of the Asian characters, too.

The Letter began life as a short story (based on an incident in real life) by W. Somerset Maugham. The story was first published in 1924 and the play version was produced in 1927: Jeanne Eagels took the lead on Broadway and Gladys Cooper in London. It is the story of Leslie Crosbie, the wife of an English rubber planter. The Crosbies have a house in the jungle, close to the plantation, but this night, the husband Bob is away, up country. So Leslie is alone. As the film begins, a white parrot is alarmed by a shot. We see a man stagger out of the plantation house. He is followed by a woman in a flowing dressing gown. She empties the gun into him. This is Leslie Crosbie. She was alone in the house, she will say, when Geoff Hammond, a neighbour came by and began to make increasingly ugly advances. So she took her husband's gun from the drawer where she knew it was kept and she shot Geoff six times.

The director is William Wyler, and he was of the opinion that Bette Davis had been getting away with too much. Take an actress of such unrestrained (possibly damaging) energies and you have to give her urgent things to do – have her firing a gun and her face can be mercifully still. Pause on it a second or two longer than is normal, and we know how to read this film and Leslie's cold, sensual face.

For many reasons, the story faced censorship problems.

The Letter

The Jeanne Eagels version had been banned in the
British Empire in part because of the treatment of
British colonials in Malaya, because the murdered man
had a Chinese mistress, and because the killer is exoner-
ated at her trial. Producer Robert Lord and writer
Howard Koch made crucial changes: the Chinese mistress became a Eurasian wife (played in haughty silence
by Gale Sondergaard), and the killer was quite definitely
punished – even if the law was an ass. Wyler asked for ten
days' private work with Koch and then a week of cast
rehearsal. Even then, he worked at his own pace, one that
Warners reckoned unduly slow. But you had only to look
at the footage to see the advantages of Wyler. *The Letter*
ended up at 95 minutes and it is brilliant.

One of its great lessons for film is that if you can
concentrate on examining character, you can almost let
plot unfold at its own pace. And *The Letter* works on this
principle: we must pay attention to every hint or sign in
Leslie Crosbie – she is that selfish and dangerous. Suppose Geoff Hammond had surprised Leslie with his
boorish advances. She shoots him once. He falls. He
seems seriously wounded. He is hardly a continuing danger. Yet she puts five more bullets in him. No, she is not
hysterical or shaking; her eyes are not all over the place.
She seems certain, implacable, resolved. Or in a trance.

The authorities are called in to investigate. We meet
the husband, Bob (Herbert Marshall), and he is effec-
tively sketched in in a couple of minutes – concerned,
tender, but stupid and unobservant. And just as Bob

hardly notices things, so the handsome wolf, the lawyer, Howard Joyce (James Stephenson), sees everything and keeps asking awkward questions. He is suspicious, or uncommitted – there is a hint that he does not like Leslie too much.

Then it is revealed. Joyce's assistant, Ong (Victor Sen Yung), has a letter, sent that night, from Leslie to Geoff, saying come and see me, saying that she is desperate. Howard now can pin Leslie as a liar and an adulteress, even a killer. He might be more vengeful or dismissive – but now we see that he may be half in love with her himself. As character deepens, the plot finds its abyss. The letter has got to be purchased, and kept out of the trial. But that financial strain ruins Bob's retirement plans. He is hurt. Leslie tries to be contrite. But then her inner being – her unhappiness – breaks out and she has to admit her debt to passion or sex – she loves the dead man, the man she killed because he didn't want her any longer. Mrs Hammond tidies up the plot and Leslie goes to her end rather in the way Julie Marsden proceeded towards the cockpit of plague in *Jezebel*. She is not forgiven. She may not be redeemed. But she has stopped lying. And if she is to be destroyed, she will manage it herself.

Once again Davis loved working with Wyler, even if she could never quite carry over his best lessons when working with other directors. They argued, but she trusted his instincts. At the moment when Leslie has to tell Bob 'I still love the man I killed', Davis was against doing it head-on into Herbert Marshall's face. But Wyler insisted and she did it his way. She shudders at the stress: 'Yes, I lost a battle,' she would write,

but I lost it to a genius. So many directors were such weak sisters that I would have to take over. Uncreative, unsure of themselves, frightened to fight back, they offered me none of the security that this tyrant did. When working, Willie – like me – could be asked, 'Whom do you hate today?' There is always something to fight in this most imperfect of worlds. Creation is hell! It's all very well for everybody to adore each other but one inevitably has to take a stand. This inevitably has to make an enemy. There is a love feast that exists on some sets – all sweetness and light and everyone tipping his hat – the ice cream industry! Everything's charming and the picture turns out to be a dud, a good, honest fight never hurt anyone and if it means a better result, so be it.

The Letter received seven Oscar nominations – for Best Picture, best actress, best supporting actor (James Stephenson), for cinematography (Tony Gaudio), for director, music and editing. It won nothing, and as for Howard Koch his impeccable work received no nod. Today, however, it is quite clear that *The Letter* is one of the finest Bette Davis pictures and an outstanding example of melodrama uncovering the nature of un-happiness. It is not so much that Leslie Crosbie is a murderess or a liar. She is a masked sensualist who can-not live openly with her desires; she does embroidery when she wants to be driven wild. She is a villainess – if you like – but she is a woman carried to the point of self-destruction by her own appetites. And the actress deserves credit not just for the very precise playing, but for the unsparing candour of the central portrait. As said at the outset, we get Mrs Crosbie and Ms Davis with equal force in that extraordinary firing of the gun. It is the most sexual gesture her career allowed her in the age of censorship. It carries the stamp of Bette Davis and her refusal to be restrained.

Confronting *The Letter* in the run of Bette Davis's pictures is ample reason for the conviction that good writing, cogent material and plausible characters are always the most likely difference between lasting movies and yesterday's dross. But just as *The Letter* was preceded by *All This, and Heaven Too*, so it is followed by *The Great Lie*. Not that the last film suffers from the deadly disadvantages of *All This*. It is fast, effective and memorable. It's just that, in the words of one of the characters, 'It is completedly mad.' *The Great Lie* is Hollywood *in extremis*, a women's picture so demented that it is not too far from being a screwball comedy. Print this section on incendiary Kleenex, please. It is also a hugely entertaining movie, and an extraordinary insight into Ms Davis.

It started life as a screenplay (based on a novel called *January Heights* by Polan Banks) by an experienced female screenwriter, Lenore Coffee. At first, as a movie project, it was called 'Far Horizon'. As such it was proposed as a Bette Davis vehicle. She read it and apparently asked that Mary Astor be offered the strong supporting part in the story. All of this came to pass. But as Astor would recount :

The story for the picture was not very strong. The first day I worked with Bette, I felt uncomfortable about it, and she sat on the set swinging her foot like a cat whipping its tail. Finally she dragged me to her dressing room and put the problem directly to me. 'Mary,' she said, 'I know you must realize that we have a perfectly lousy story the way it stands now. We've got to do something about it, and between us I think we can.'

Others report that that is how *The Great Lie* (as it became known) advanced. The two actresses frequently halted the shooting to repair the script, and the director Edmund Goulding ostentatiously lounged around waiting for their pages and their instruction. In which case, we owe it to Ms Davis to spell out just what happens in this loony film.

Peter Van Allen (George Brent – it's that manikin, again) wakes up, hung-over, in a Manhattan apartment smashed to pieces. There was a party. His new wife, Sandra Kovac (Mary Astor), a great concert pianist, is still sleeping. Peter, even hung-over, begins to wonder why he married her. His lawyer tells him that the marriage is actually null and void: her previous divorce had not come through in time. Like an honourable chump, he says he will marry her again anyway – next Tuesday. She's playing in Philadelphia that day, she protests.

So Peter flies (he is a flier!) off to Maryland and the lovely country home of Maggie Patterson (Bette Davis), the woman he really loves. Tuesday, Sandra is a no-show, so Peter marries Maggie – he is drinking all the time. She encourages him to follow his flying career (it might be useful to the government!). But flying over the South American jungle he crashes and is lost. (Is this the end of George Brent again?) Whereupon, Sandra reveals that she is pregnant, as in 'with child'. Those party nights with Peter were not entirely empty – unless you believe in conception by other means (like listening to her play Tchaikovsky).

Please take a deep, steady breath: Maggie now makes this proposition. Sandra has and wants a life of travel, concert dates, cocktails and Tchaikovsky. She doesn't need a baby. But Maggie does. For a cash dispensation, she 'buys' the baby and acts as if it was always hers – born on a trip to the Grand Canyon. I am not making this up. But Davis and Astor may have done so.

Do not trust the jungles of South America. Lost fliers have a way of staggering back to civilization. In this case, a research botanist named Potts seems to have been the rescuing agent – whatever, with only a streak of gray in his black Irish hair, Peter Van Allen comes striding back into view. Of course, he is delighted to meet 'little Pete', and that dread Hollywood terminus – a happy life – is clear on the horizon. But then Sandra reappears. She says she wants the baby, but it's clear she really yearns for a full-grown Peter. She threatens Maggie, but then the plucky Maryland girl says enough of lies and pretence, let the truth be told. She tells Peter everything, and like a noble soul he says, very well, alas, the babe must go with Sandra, but I'm staying in Maryland. This ending seems rushed at first viewing, but then it dawns on you that the frantic speed is essential. Sandra sighs and gives up the baby. Instead, she collapses at a piano and begins to pound out Tchaikovsky as if it were her drug and her life.

With fabulous clothes and brimming emotional close-ups, the game of *The Great Lie* is played with zest, and the lunatic exhilaration of the plot is rapid enough for us to realize quite slowly that the attitude to babies and music is scatterbrained. In a shrewd account of the film, Jeanine Basinger concludes, 'Davis, the perfect mother, wins back both of her two children, father and son. Perfection in motherhood can exist only when cut loose from a sexual desire like Astor's, and when the woman's primary interest is in possessing the child.'

That's a great insight and one that points to the way the conventions of the women's picture are so urgent in trying to separate sexuality and the family spirit. But Basinger might have gone further in assessing a film that we are told the leading women took over. At the time of *The Great Lie*, Bette Davis had just married Arthur Farnsworth (the flier!) and was facing the conflict between New England and Hollywood (Maryland

or New York in the movie). Mary Astor was coming to
the end of her third marriage, but she had just had a
child. The screwball bent I referred to comes in the hysterical stress on the code of the women's picture – it
doesn't reach the surrealism of a kind of tennis where
the baby is the ball. But the narrative spasms are the
signs of an attitude that cannot place or feel the lives of
children, but which has learned how to see the pyro-
technics of performance (acting or playing the piano)
as a metaphor for sexual activity.

One reason why *The Great Lie* is so watchable is the
undoubted rapport between Davis and Astor. All too
often in her pictures, we feel a chill between Bette and
her female co-stars (Miriam Hopkins is the clearest victim, or instigator, of this). But Davis and Astor play like
good friends, and it's easy to believe that Bette was
always encouraging Mary towards the supporting actress
Oscar that she won. Astor seems taller than Davis – and
taller than was the case. Time and again they are shot in
rhythm, and in their conversations there is the equality
and admiration of respectful gunslingers in a man's
world. At the time, much was made of the realism with
which Astor had learned to play the piano. What is still
evident is her sensual confidence at the keys and the
way the surging motions of concerto-making are like
lovemaking for her. In turn, this helps us recognize
anew the frantic passion that Bette brings to the thing
she'd call acting. The real lie is that either of these two
women is ever going to be held and fulfilled by ideas of

little Pete and Maryland. But isn't it pretty to think so? The true ugliness of Leslie Crosbie is that the possibility of a child has never crossed her mind.

Warners had cast Davis once before with Jimmy Cagney — in *Jimmy the Gent*, but that was in another age. So you can understand everyone involved thinking that the noisiest contract players at the studio might make a screwball team, neither one afraid of or quite listening to the other. The result was *The Bride Came C.O.D.* based on a screenplay by Philip and Julius Epstein, about an heiress and a pilot. It was the kind of light-hearted project that would have had a better chance with younger players itching for a break. Cagney and Davis looked too old for the fun, and it was proved yet again that the two Warner powerhouses were very difficult to play with.

But then, another sudden reversal, and perhaps the best piece of material Bette ever had in her years at Warner Brothers. Yet this was not a Warners film. Lillian Hellman's play, *The Little Foxes*, had opened in 1939 with Tallulah Bankhead as Regina Giddens, who outwits her two rascal brothers in a business deal. Hellman said that it was based on her own family history, but the play was a very effective Southern melodrama, and one of those key American works arguing that money means more than family ties.

Born in Alabama, Bankhead had had an immense personal success as Regina — though director Herman Shumlin had had to work hard to persuade her to be

Regina instead of Tallulah. But the actress stuck at it and she obtained the best reviews of her career, as well as 10 per cent of the gross (the show ran over 400 performances). It was a tough play in that it had no substantial character anyone could like. But Samuel Goldwyn admired the play and was determined to make it, with William Wyler directing. It was Wyler who urged Goldwyn to get Bette Davis for Regina. But everyone knew that Warners had a rule with their difficult actress – she was not to be loaned out.

But money was working. In her book, Davis claims that Goldwyn paid her $385,000 to play Regina. That is an outlandish sum, way beyond Davis's rate and not confirmed in other accounts. But there was an extra pressure: Warners were mounting *Sergeant York* for producer Jesse Lasky, and that project was desperate to have Gary Cooper who was under contract to Goldwyn. There were talks, but they only came to fruition when Goldwyn said that, for a Davis–Cooper swap on one picture, he might also waive a personal gambling debt that Jack Warner owed to Goldwyn – perhaps as much as $425,000. The deal was done, and no one now knows for sure how much Bette pocketed. I doubt she was as decisive or as successful as Regina, but it's probable that she was paid more than she had ever received before.

Goldwyn also asked Hellman to soften the play. The role of the daughter would be built up – she had a boyfriend now, a newspaper writer, and a sceptical observer of the Hubbard–Giddens control of the Southern town.

The Little Foxes

Teresa Wright would play the daughter and newcomer Richard Carlson made a nice debut as her boyfriend. Davis had seen and admired Bankhead's performance, and she was dismayed that Wyler wanted her to find a new way of playing it. Wyler saw Regina as a hardened woman, not just a bitch but a monster, and he wanted Bette to look rather older than her real age.

This clearly made for trouble. Bette was compelled to use a whitewash make-up based on rice, and Wyler then asked Gregg Toland to film her so that the age shone through. There are mirror scenes in the film where Regina (and Bette) is forced to survey her own loss of beauty or youth. Davis plays them to the hilt, but that was not her first inclination. Indeed, it's clear that there was a hold-up on the film when director and actress quarrelled and when Wyler talked of starting again with Bankhead. That must have been bullying talk, especially at Bette's high pay rate, but it led to Davis saying aloud that she was very unhappy with her performance.

History shows no sympathy for her opinion. *The Little Foxes* is by far the most successful Hellman adaptation to the screen, and in large part this is because of the way Wyler and Toland conceived of a visual style to match the claustrophobic power-plays of the stage original. *The Little Foxes* was the first picture Toland had shot after *Citizen Kane*. It is nowhere near as spectacular or innovative a film. But it shows a professional director like Wyler studying deep-focus photography and finding a very literal use for it. So the Giddens house is a cockpit in which all things are happening simultaneously. This enhances realism and relationship, yet it sharpens melodrama, too – so as we see Regina, serene but unyielding in the background, we watch her husband, Horace (Herbert Marshall again), struggling to get the heart medicine that can save his life.

This visual design is absorbing, and for the ordinary viewer it may have been more cogent than the extraordinary poetic use of depth in *Kane*. But it meant that the film relied on ensemble playing – and four of the cast (Carl Benton Reid, Charles Dingle, Patricia Collinge and Dan Duryea) all came from the stage production. So we feel the stale familiarity and self-loathing of this family, and we feel trapped in the lush but rotting spaces of the house. Regina runs the action, but only in the way a queen rat might dominate her tribe. It is less a star vehicle than a venture into the toxic infection of modern American capitalism and the way in which sentiment has been brutally converted into cash. Unrelenting at 116 minutes, and withering in its sense that the greedy Regina has lost the love of her daughter for money, it is a foreboding portrait of America made in the era of war such as only reveals the vitality and courage of the country.

Moreover, *The Little Foxes* turned out a hit. Audiences went to see it, and the film was nominated for nine Oscars, the same number as received by *Kane* in the same year. Of course, neither film did well: *Kane* won the Oscar for screenplay – and that was the only victory between the two films. Toland's photography was nominated, but only for *Kane*. Bette was nominated, and both Teresa Wright and Patricia Collinge were nominated for supporting actress. The wins in those categories went to Joan Fontaine in *Suspicion*, and Mary Astor in *The Great Lie*. I enjoy Astor in that film as much as anyone, but to say that she is less touching and lifelike than Patrica Collinge in *The Little Foxes* is foolish. Worse still, would be to claim that Davis is 'better' than Agnes Moorehead in *Kane* or *The Magnificent Ambersons* (neither of which performances was even nominated).

Of course, Agnes Moorehead was not exactly a movie star – not quite. But Davis's performance as Regina forces the comparison if only because Bette is playing period and family. No matter the fights behind the scenes, Bette Davis is at her best in *The Little Foxes*, never asking for pity or excuse, never flinching from the raw greed in Regina. But Agnes Moorehead was existing at a quite different level of psychological realism – as a person hardly noticed outside her own home. No one would have asked such a thing of Bette Davis.

In 1942, as the '41 Oscars were awarded, Bette Davis was still only thirty-four. She was at her peak, with two Oscars and three more nominations. She had made forty-six pictures in eleven years, and she was the leading actress in the movie world (in the same period, Joan Crawford had made twenty-four, Katharine Hepburn had done nineteen pictures – and Garbo had only nine). Those numbers are startling and they remind us of the unflagging rate of Bette's energy – as well as her modest capacity for private life. Most of the pictures identified as hers had been hits. It was a measure of this reputation that Davis was elected as the first female president of the Academy. This was an honorary award, but Bette took it with customary earnestness. She studied the Academy laws and began a programme of reform before others indicated that that much participation was not expected. So she resigned. But then, with John Garfield, she formed and really worked at the Hollywood Canteen, an entertainment centre for US servicemen.

Her pace did not seem affected at first, but in the years 1942–46 she would only make another seven films. Moreover, in 1945 she undertook her third marriage and in 1947, at the age of thirty-nine, she had her first child. In addition, in the summer of 1943, Joan Crawford was released by MGM and signed on by Warners. She was set to make three films for her new studio for $500,000. By then, Bette was earning at a higher rate, but the rivalry was quite clear. Although a year older than Bette, Joan had the edge in looks and glamour. Both were idolized by large female audiences. But Bette had allowed herself to be cast in a great many period pictures, while Joan strove to be the modern independent woman. *Mildred Pierce* was the picture that relaunched Joan's career, but that book had been bought by Warners long before Crawford arrived in Burbank, and it was clearly considered first as a Bette Davis vehicle. Bette could have played the part for sure, but could she have captured Crawford's sense of the post-war

American woman on her own and counting every penny? Would her Mildred have been as vulnerable to her own daughter, Veda, as Crawford's proved to be?

The writer is at your service, of course; and so he should be. But bear with his labouring spirit a moment, for just to give you a few hundred words – to the point, but pointed – he is seeing every Bette Davis film again. To be precise, he has just suffered through *The Man Who Came to Dinner*. You may hear in the dark fields of the republic that this is an old favourite of the repertory theatre circuits. Do not be deceived – it is a reason to commit murder.

Moss Hart and George Kaufman wrote it as a play and it ran over 700 performances in 1939–40. So great was its fame that Warners had to pay $250,000 for the movie rights! The first thought on stage had been that the poorly disguised portrait of Alexander Woolcott – wit and monster – was ready-made for John Barrymore. Alas, that actor was too far gone in drink to carry it off, and Monty Woolley got the part instead. Woolley was an acting teacher who became an actor. You hear sometimes that there are some who love him. I think he is fit to be throttled in mid-sentence, and so sentimental that he misses the strange mixture of genius and hatefulness that sparked Woolcott and which is really needed for the role.

Warners gave the script assignment to the Epsteins and then found that Bette Davis wanted to play the part of Maggie Cutler, secretary to Sheridan Whiteside. The pretext for play and film alike is that Whiteside – author, broadcaster and ego – is touring the provinces. He has agreed to dine with a humble couple but slips on their icy steps and is compelled to rest in the innocent home. He then finds that he risks losing Maggie to a local newspaper man who looks and sounds a lot like Ralph Bellamy in *His Girl Friday*.

Davis begged for Barrymore to get the role in the film, and the great man did a screen test that was pathetic. Of course, the sensible thing then would have been to have Bette play Whiteside herself with the Maggie role flipped into a caustic male secretary (George Brent?). Instead, Davis went ahead with the film with Woolley, and she demonstrates that she can indeed stand around doing very little except chuckling at her own jokes and wearing a few pert hats. It is not enough. I have warned you and I do not mean to upset myself any further by saying more for the uncommon strain of *Mr Skeffington* is coming up, and a writer needs to be prepared for that bit of brandy on the high wire. There are only a few Bette Davis pictures from her prime years completed without reason, interest or mischief – *The Man Who Came to Dinner* is the classic.

But if that apparent indifference tempted you to think that Bette Davis had gone cool on acting, or on herself, wait one minute. Her next film, all the more remarkable for being so neglected, is hair-raising. *In This Our Life* is the second film directed by John Huston, and if it is not as compelling or tidy as the first, *The Maltese Falcon*, still the two together present an alarming portrait of the young Huston's nihilism and his greedy eye for unpleasant people. It came from a Pulitzer prize-winning novel by Ellen Glasgow, and from a script by Howard Koch (who had done *The Letter*). As such, it was plainly intended as a Davis vehicle. So attend to its arresting story.

We are in some small Southern town. Stanley Timberlake (Bette Davis) is a wide-eyed flirt, a rampant narcissist and a very dangerous woman. She seduces the husband (Dennis Morgan) of her sister, Roy (Olivia de Havilland), goes off with him and then promotes the circumstances in which he commits suicide. More or less, this transgression seems to be overlooked. Stanley comes back. She is close to seducing her rich uncle (Charles Coburn), and taking her sister's new boyfriend (George Brent). But then she kills a child in a hit-and-run accident and tries to blame a young black man who works for the family. This may be the nastiest Bette we have ever seen, the most loathsome, and she is flying on pale wings of self-love.

It is a very uneasy film. Several things strain credulity and the relationship between sisters Roy and Stanley is all the stranger because Huston was infatuated with de Havilland (this shows in the Ernest Haller photography) and so in awe of Bette's freed spite that he stood back and gave her her head. 'She has a demon within her,' Huston would write, 'which threatens to break out and eat everybody.' It is also a wartime film in which America seems destabilized by its own inner diseases – like racism: the young black man, articulate and smart, is an unprecedentedly modern character.

But if you want one more clinching reason for treating this wild beast of a film more carefully, try this: in 1933, John Huston had killed a woman in a driving accident in Los Angeles. The matter had been hushed up so as not to slow his promising career – and Hollywood was a little like the South in those days, its own private kingdom. But it remains an unasked and unanswered question as to how far Huston was addressing his own old guilt in this very frightening film. The best compliment I can give Davis is to say that she is so aroused by Stanley's evil that she seems several years younger than her real age.

Yet again, the Davis pendulum swings wildly as we come to her next film, *Now, Voyager*, perhaps the film that made the deepest impression on her fans. Take the two Davis characters in her previous films – Maggie Cutler and Stanley Timberlake. Maggie is of service to others. She is quiet, self-effacing, deferential, well behaved. Stanley is nearly demented by personal desire and ambition. Suppose, for the sake of argument, that a sociologist in the early 1940s had offered Maggie and Stanley as alternate role models or warning figures in a woman's life. How is the struggle between the two of them to be resolved?

The project came from a novel by Olive Higgins

Prouty, and it dealt with the coming to life and liberty of a woman named Charlotte Vale. She begins, in spectacles and tightly bunned hair, as a spinster figure, the daughter intimidated by a sophisticated and cunning mother (Gladys Cooper), an early casualty to life's fears. But then Charlotte meets a psychiatrist, Dr Jaquith (Claude Rains), who has to rescue her from a nervous breakdown. Emerging from her old self, she meets a married man, Jerry Durrance (Paul Henreid), and falls in love with him. In time, Charlotte will help Jerry's daughter (Janis Wilson) with her emotional problems and so Charlotte and Jerry end the film, smoking the same cigarette together with her telling him, 'Don't let's ask for the moon. We have the stars.'

Bette challenged the studio's first inclination, that Irene Dunne be hired in to play Charlotte. Norma Shearer and Ginger Rogers were also considered. But Bette took the part over and in her book she claims that she was in close contact with Olive Higgins Prouty on the script. Casey Robinson, who wrote the script, denied that and says that the production – under a newcomer, director Irving Rapper – moved forward smoothly, but never allowed a hint that Charlotte and Jerry had actually had a sexual affair. In those days, of course, complicity on screen with a cigarette might be thought to bypass more awkward realities. A Stanley Timberlake might have sneered at such discretion, but *Now, Voyager* is far more decorous and polite a film than *In This Our Life*. Its real aim is to keep a plausible level of life while hinting at the characters' fantasies. Indeed, Davis would say later that she did not think Charlotte and Jerry would ever get together. It was more likely that her character would end up with Dr Jaquith, helping him in his work and confirming the value of infant (or infantile) psychotherapy for the unhappy woman. It is in the nature of the women's picture that its recommendations extend from that kind of marginal emergence of the buried self to bold gestures of murder and triumph in the hypocritical world. Bette could play it either way, and either way *Now, Voyager* is the legend for women who believe in their as yet undiscovered being and the perfect man who will feel its existence.

Now, Voyager was a hit, with domestic rentals over $2 million. The picture was not nominated, but Bette got her fifth best actress nod in a row – *Jezebel*; *Dark Victory*; *The Letter*; *The Little Foxes*; *Now, Voyager* – a remarkable line that shows how far her own giddy extremism was her friend with audiences. American women loved to love her, and to pretend they might be as brave or reckless as she was. But they got the same amount of satisfaction when they could disapprove of her. That simple fact says everything about the appeal of Bette Davis in the great age of movie dreaming.

But war was now the central focus, and Bette regarded the Hollywood Canteen as her baby. In a nationwide tour Davis spearheaded the sale of $2 million in war bonds, and in Los Angeles she was a regular, helping out at the Canteen on La Cienega. Of course, a lot of movie stars helped with this, but no one took it more seriously than Bette. She also appeared in a couple of 'canteen' movies – *Thank Your Lucky Stars*, where she sings 'They're Either Too Young or Too Old', and dances the jitterbug with a young champion. The next year, she and John Garfield were prominent in the picture, *Hollywood Canteen*. They were both Warners names, yet they had never really worked together – they are both in *Juarez* but not on screen together. It's worth noting that Garfield would soon play the violinist opposite Joan Crawford in *Humoresque* (a film worthy of Davis), and not very long after that he was a blacklisted outcast brought to an early death.

In addition, Davis contributed herself to the filming of *Watch on the Rhine*. This was a play, by Lillian Hellman, premiered in April 1941, about an American household that happens to be entertaining a Nazi and an anti-fascist at the same time. The play and the subsequent film (both directed by Herman Shumlin) are very talky, earnest and pained – and the emotional event was enough to win the Oscar for Paul Lukas, who played the anti-fascist on stage and screen. For the movie, Bette Davis filled the role of the wife (taken by Mady Christians on stage). It is not a large role, but Davis plays it with quiet conviction, and it is likely that her presence prompted the film to be seen by many more people than might otherwise have been the case.

Watch on the Rhine has strenuous, sententious speeches such as war may explain – but not excuse. The best

American war pictures are those in which the nation and its ideas are defended by smart, idiomatic conversation, and robust tolerance – and talk is often one of the sweetest fruits of a democracy. There's one 'war' scene in *Old Acquaintance*, where the Bette Davis character speaks up for the war effort, and it's fine. But she serves the cause better simply by observing life with sad intelligence. And whereas *Watch on the Rhine* is close to soporific, *Old Acquaintance* is a small delight, and one of those films in which Bette herself comes across as deeply likeable.

Kit Marlowe (Davis) is a writer – of literate, mid-list books that do not sell. She is admired and envied by a childhood friend, Millie Drake (Miriam Hopkins), a vain, rather stupid woman who has the common touch Kit lacks and who turns herself into a queen of the novelette. Millie has a husband, Pres (John Loder – in the best thing he ever did), melancholy, a little drunk and in love with the quiet, calm, insightful Kit. He proposes to Kit and of course she says no, so Pres drifts away.

Ten years pass: Millie is now a rich sensation – Kit is out of print. But Kit is looking after Deirdre (Dolores Moran), the daughter to Millie and Pres. Of course, Pres comes back. There is another man (a young Gig Young – five years Bette's junior, but feeling younger still), and finally the two women are left as old, but weary friends. Kit is one of those whose life has passed her by, but she is a champ of kindness and decency and a few people know it.

It all comes from a play by John Van Druten, and he

and Lenore Coffee did the screenplay. Vincent Sherman (hot off *The Hard Way*) was chosen to direct it, and I suspect that a lot of the film's wit and finesse are due to him. The stories are still told of the upstaging battles between Hopkins and Davis, and of how artfully they manipulated each other until Sherman took charge. It's hard to see Bette as that defenceless – and on screen Davis handles her co-star like Robinson knocking out La Motta. But Sherman has described what a difficult piece it was for Bette. This was the time of Farney's death and of Bette's confusion. Sherman told a story about how, driving him home after work, Bette stopped the car and told Sherman she loved him. He thought it was conventional showbiz talk, but then she convinced him. And lo and behold there's a matching scene in the picture where Pres says the same thing to Kit while she's talking on the phone. There was an affair with Sherman, and yet again you feel a ruefulness creeping into the Davis eyes but growing older with silver flair in her hair, and the unstoppable passage of time.

Decades later, *Old Acquaintance* was remade by George Cukor as *Rich and Famous*, with Jacqueline Bisset and Candice Bergen. The original is far superior, funny, touching and unexpectedly grown-up, and it might be better still if it had bothered to trace the divergent writing styles of the two authors. But time and again, in the face of the old Miriam Hopkins bluster, Bette Davis lets us know that she had it in her to be a seriously modest, controlled figure – just the kind of character Kit

Marlowe must have written about. The fascinating thing is that there is more offered, suggestively, about human values in terms of how people behave than in all the set-piece lectures of *Watch on the Rhine*.

Which brings us to *Mr Skeffington*, the last film of the war era, and one of the most intriguing. We begin in New York City on the eve of the First World War. Gentlemen arrive for a dinner party at the Trellis house. They are all suitors for the hand of Fanny (Bette Davis), except for one visitor, not invited – Job Skeffington (Claude Rains), an investment broker and until lately the employer of Fanny's brother, Trippy. He brings news that Trippy (not a good name to have in a film of this kind) has swindled the company of $24,000. Skeffington is Jewish – the name was Skarvinsky once – and there is from the outset an edge of suspicion towards him.

The story came from a novel by Elizabeth von Arnim, and it was purchased in 1941, a few years before it was made. When offered to Bette Davis at that time, she declined – Fanny would have to be fifty or so in the major part of the action and Davis said that was out of her reach. But the novel was taken up by the Epstein brothers. They liked it so much that they became producers of the project – and they waited for Davis. It was their ambition to make one of the first American mainstream feature films that took American anti-Semitism for granted.

As the story works out, Fanny marries Job (in a drab New Jersey Justice of the Peace's home) to avoid scandal for Trippy. But that weak brother is killed in the war. Job and Fanny have a daughter (Marjorie Riordan), but their marriage breaks down. As the years pass, Job goes to Europe. At close to fifty, Fanny has diphtheria and loses her looks. Job returns. He has been in a concentration camp, and he is blind now. He thinks she is as lovely as ever, and so she looks after him.

The opportunity for socal commentary and irony is fairly clear. This could be a chilling picture – all the more striking in coming out of the US at the end of the war. It's hardly surprising that much of this is muffled, though Jack Warner himself was of the opinion that – carried away with ambition – the Epsteins had themselves created too many unnecessary scenes – the picture was released at 146 minutes which is at least thirty too many.

In addition, by his own account, director Vincent Sherman was having to console his lead actress – in bed – every few days during the shooting. He was that doormat after the death of Fanny. Moreover, even as the young Fanny, Davis wore ringlets – not the best way of piling her wavy hair – so that there is not enough contrast in the ageing process. We should feel that raw selfishness has changed her face as much as anything else. And the ending would play better still if Fanny had been scarred by illness.

On the other hand, Claude Rains is outstanding as Skeffington – dry, suave, very practical, yet with a guarded well of love in him, too. Davis aways said she relished playing with Rains (they did four films together), yet she might be more alert to him in *Mr Skeffington*, and more gradually made aware of his moral intelligence and the complex pact she has with her husband in terms of reputation and standard of living.

Mr Skeffington needed Wyler's toughness, more economy and a wiser way with Bette's hair and make-up. The film did well enough, and it won Oscar nominations for Bette and Claude Rains – her seventh, his third. But it's hard to watch now without feeling an urge to improve it.

In 1945, Bette Davis married for the third time. At a party in Laguna del Mar, she met a good-looking man just out of the Navy. His name was William Grant Sherry, and he was trying to be a painter. 'What did she do?' he asked. We can imagine her eyes widening, uncertain how much she was being teased. Is it possible in 1945, in a world where movie stars had far more authority than they have now, that this fellow really didn't recognize Bette Davis? Or was he clever enough to divine how much that unlikely response would attract her? He came from real poverty, it turned out – his mother was an elevator operator. So they were married, no matter that Bette's mother disliked him intensely. They honeymooned in Mexico, but on the way driving there, in an argument, he threw her out of the car. In Mexico, he threw a trunk at her.

I cannot say that Sherry and I did not have a stimulating relationship. He matched me in temperament all the way. I would say that I trailed him in this department. He wanted to be indispensable to me and that, of course, was impossible. Though industrious and pitiably contrite after his outbursts, Sherry's dedication as an artist fell far short of mine and his frustrations had a frenzy that terrorized me.

On 1 May 1947, Bette gave birth by Caesarean section to Barbara Davis Sherry (thereafter generally known as B.D.). At the same time, the doctors told her she could not have another child. It marked a difference: 'I had no desire to give up my career but somehow it didn't matter as much. My life seemed full without it. I had won my battle. I had reached my peak – inside.'

Bette remained at Warners, and she was told by the studio that she could be like a producer on her projects. But in the event she was allowed – or she took – very little power, and in the late '40s any observer could be forgiven for thinking that Davis had lost interest, or that the public found it difficult to place her in the post-war landscape.

Not that that horizon was empty of interesting women: Barbara Stanwyck (a year older than Bette) had altered the way she was perceived with *Double Indemnity*, *The Strange Love of Martha Ivers* and *Sorry, Wrong Number*; Joan Crawford found new life with *Mildred Pierce*, *Humoresque*, *Possessed*, *Daisy Kenyon*, *Flamingo Road* and *Sudden Fear* (she got three nominations in that package). Olivia de Havilland had the best run of her life: *To Each His Own*, *The Snake Pit*, *The Heiress*; and Jane Wyman became another new star at Warners.

It's a game, but an interesting game, to wonder in which of those roles Davis could have excelled – all the Crawford parts, surely, as well as *The Heiress* and *Sorry, Wrong Number*. When we look at Katharine Hepburn in the same years we see *State of the Union*, *Adam's Rib* and *The African Queen* (and once upon a time Davis had been in line to play Rose). Ingrid Bergman had done *Notorious*, *Arch of Triumph* and *Joan of Arc*. And at the end of the decade Gloria Swanson was brought back from retirement to play in *Sunset Boulevard*.

Against those careers, Bette Davis did *The Corn is Green*, *A Stolen Life*, *Deception*, *Winter Meeting*, *June Bride* and *Beyond the Forest* – the last one so extreme and, as she thought, misguided that it prompted Davis to quit Warners, the studio where she had been for over twenty-five years. Henry Blanke produced four of those post-war films, and he was a good man. He had done *Jezebel*, and while he was with Bette he also did *The Treasure of the Sierra Madre* and *The Fountainhead*. Was he waiting for Bette to be more the producer? Was she suddenly lost when she tried to judge the public's fresh appetite for material? How many stories does Hollywood ever encourage or understand about women passing forty (it appears to have been a far more sinister and damning pact than being close to the Communist Party)?

Nevertheless, the post-war films have a crazed quality, as if to suggest that no one was in charge. *Deception* is said to have turned a small profit, on costs of $2 million (with Bette herself at $7,000 a week), yet it only seems plausible as part of a demented feud between Davis and Crawford. This isn't far-fetched: if your studio has those two ladies at the same time, it's almost inevitable that you present them as being in a contest. Apparently, Crawford and her producer Jerry Wald had their musical picture lined up first: *Humoresque*, with Joan as a society woman fatally in love with a violin genius (played by John Garfield). It's that old story of talent and art meaning more to the man than love can be for the woman. So Bette found *Deception* in retaliation. I'm going to try to tell you the story of *Deception* – but it may be more than any of us can handle.

There has been a war in Europe, a great calamity. But Karel Novak (Paul Henreid) has survived with all his fingers so that he can be the genius of the cello. Christina Radcliffe (Bette Davis) loves him. But why, he wonders, is she living in this immense apartment (designed by Anton Grot) when she is only a music teacher? Ah, she sighs, and welcomes him in. But she had her war, too, not in conflict, but trying to keep a straight face while Claude Rains overacted as Alexander Holenius, a very great composer (and vile show-off) . . . who happens to have a cello concerto ready.

It ends badly, though Novak plays the concerto and Holenius is dead. The film is dreadful – and it is just a few years before *All About Eve*, a model of wit, taste and knowingness. What makes matters far worse is that in *Deception* the characters simply sit around and talk.

Nothing happens. The high point of the film involves a very swish Rains ordering an absurd dinner for the three of them. But, you might say, and presumably the public said so, isn't this the trio of players from *Now, Voyager*? Yes, but without a script or a storyline. By contrast, *Humoresque* – which was never meant to be treated as a dry exercise – is a classically well-made film. There are stories of skirmishes on the Warners lot in the late '40s between Crawford and Davis over men, dressing-room facilities and ridiculous statements. But nothing alters the fact that Crawford was making better and far more suitable films. Moreover, it's clear that someone – most likely Bette herself – had made the changes in the play on which *Deception* is based. That's all very well, if the changes are improvements. From *The Letter* to *Deception* is six years, yet in that time a star has become a liability and without any grasp of how her decline has happened.

Then something in the beast stirs. It's nothing too reliable, for Bette Davis went out of her way to tell the world that she hated *Beyond the Forest*, and the film has become known as a piece of camp mockery: Rosa Moline's line, 'What a dump!' when she enters her own home, was adopted by Edward Albee as the opening line of *Who's Afraid of Virginia Woolf*? But the quoter – Martha – can't even recall the name of the picture. Well, now it's notorious, like an item in Trivial Pursuit. Yet nobody knows that the film is extraordinary, or beyond its actress's understanding.

But who can be expected to understand *Beyond the Forest* when it has an opening title completely at odds with its desperate protagonist. 'This is the story of evil . . . ' it begins, with further collective prayers about how, sometimes, looking at evil can be useful if just as a warning. What is this about? Rosa Moline is a murderess, an adulteress, a wilful aborter of her own child, and she has terrible hair. But evil? Or is this just the shield of Warner Brothers trying to stand up to the arrows of the League of Decency, which condemned *Beyond the Forest*?

There are films about evil people, where the alleged element of 'warning' is a cover for making a lot of money. But Rosa Moline doesn't fit the very tidy handling of, say, Hannibal Lecter in *The Silence of the Lambs*. Rosa is unique unto herself, her social predicament and the relentless urgings of Bette Davis cut with some sense of her resembling Flaubert's Emma Bovary.

Beyond the Forest was a novel, by Stuart Engstrand, scripted by Lenore Coffee. The film was directed by King Vidor – perhaps Davis's first encounter with a great director, by which I mean a pronounced visual stylist, easily drawn to extremes. (Vidor's previous film had been *The Fountainhead*.) Rosa Moline is the doctor's wife in a small, dull, lumber town, Loyalton, Wisconsin. She looks like nothing on earth. And this is very rare for Bette Davis who, throughout her career, enjoyed the fond attentions of costumier Orry-Kelly, and nearly always seemed very smartly turned out.

Rosa is a mess. She wears wide skirts, low-slung

blouses and high-heeled shoes. Her hair is dark and long. There is a gypsy look, sometimes, but then we see her housemaid — a full Indian — and we wonder what unholy mix of blood Rosa may be. More than that, she dresses inappropriately — the wrong clothes in the wrong scene (Edith Head did the costumes and one longs to hear her rationale — or the horrified yielding to Vidor's raw vision). Rosa wants life, fun, wealth, she wants Chicago — and the train to that city is like the locomotive in *Anna Karenina*, a nemesis.

The reference to Emma Bovary occurs in the novel apparently, and despite her savagery it is possible to see Rosa as a constantly thwarted romantic spirit. She behaves terribly — yet her trashy violence is not that far from camp daredevil. She hopes that the confusion will be excused and explained by her terrible yearning. In short, wretched behaviour as a measure of integrity. Yes, she is destructive; yes, she is insane, and very dangerous to others. But two things sustain Rosa: our understanding that Emma Bovaries do long to get away, even if the going may destroy them; and the weird commitment from Davis to this wild creature. By the end of the film, I think, one reappraises the way Edward Albee chose that line. It wasn't chance. It's a way of getting at the fears and failure that fill Martha's life. Now, Martha is drunk, a loud-mouth, a scene-maker, someone you might work hard to avoid. But Rosa Moline is worse. She is the rogue insurrectionary that polite society is going to have to put down.

Beyond the Forest was a disaster. It surely helped bring about the break between Davis and Warner Brothers — though aiding that may have counted as a kindness. It is also — because of Vidor's eye and his instinct for self-destructive liberty — one of the best films Bette Davis ever made, a film that leaves Charlotte Vale and Judith Traherne seeming insipid and genteel. It is also a sign of how far the poetry of silent film, or the violence of opera, lay close to Davis's heart. It is the unmistakable work of an actress who scorns naturalism. And it is one more proof that we need to watch her very closely and never take anything for granted. Just as it was the end of Warner Brothers for Bette, so it is the moment before her most famous film, the one that everybody thinks they understand, the one in which she seems in charge of the show.

Her third marriage, the one to William Grant Sherry, ended with talk of his personal violence. He had signed an agreement that he would seek no money from her. But he was broke and thus he made a public confession about his violent behaviour in an attempt to soften her heart. The press decided that there must be two sides to the whole business, and there was talk that Bette had been involved with co-star Barry Sullivan on *Payment on Demand*. No more marriage! she announced.

Then, in April 1949, while filming a rape attack scene in *Three Came Home*, Claudette Colbert injured her back. It was a ruptured disk. She cried out with pain, and with fury and frustration because she realized that she would probably miss the role of Margo Channing in *All About Eve* which had been offered to her. It was a story about the theatre, one in which a novice actress, Eve Harrington, moves in on the territory of a real star, Margo, apparently overwhelmed by admiration and reverence, but driven to take over her position. Or rather, that is the pretext for the game. In fact, as Pauline Kael observed, it's hard to credit that this Eve is a threat to Margo.

In writer-director Joseph L. Mankiewicz's screenplay it was stressed that Eve and Margo looked alike, and the nice thing about Claudette Colbert and Anne Baxter was their resemblance. Mankiewicz was foreseeing ways of capturing it on film.

Once it was clear that Colbert was disabled, the studio, Twentieth Century-Fox, thought of Marlene Dietrich or Susan Hayward for Margo. Gertrude Lawrence was offered the part. But just days before shooting began, Bette Davis signed on – at $130,000 for twelve weeks' work.

In just a few years, Bette Davis had put on weight and let her hair grow longer. Truth to tell, in *All About Eve*, she looks more than her forty-two, but Mankiewicz was ready to let Margo's age slide forward. Edith Head dressed the actress as kindly as possible, but the asset that we all associate with Margo is what she has to say and the intricate, bittersweet cleverness of *All About Eve* is its view of a contest in which there is always a new young kid staring as if transfixed at

stardom. Margo is vulnerable, temperamental and prob-
lematic, but gently so. She is also wiser, kinder and far
more sporting than the grasping Eve. Margo is the sympathetic part who is able to survey the theatre and its
antics with dry amusement. She has seen it all – except
for the flagrant nerve of this copycat thief. And if Eve
gets what she wants – stardom – still, along the way, she
has made a fatal bargain with the serpent himself, the
sardonic theatre columnist Addison de Witt (George
Sanders). Whereas Margo is left secure with her husband and director, Bill Sampson (played by the rugged
actor Gary Merrill).

I am sure Claudette Colbert would have been fine.
But Bette is forever Margo Channing, a spiteful Peking-
ese peeping out of the high collar of a fur coat and the
inspired troublemaker promising the assembly, 'It's
going to be a bumpy night.' She surveys Anne Baxter
and even Marilyn Monroe with an effortless authority,
understanding these kids' games better than anyone
else. Margo is not a difficult part. It is a softball waiting
to be hit out of the park. Bette behaved herself during
the filming and she was smart enough to know she had
never had such lines before. Moreover, for someone
who had never quite dared to be 'beautiful', Davis had
now established herself in the most awkward terrain
for an actress – that of middle age. Alas, she hardly
realized the deepest lesson: that middle-aged women
can get away with movies if they have great lines to
deliver – or if the things theatre-people say in life are as

All About Eve

bright and cutting as the knives they toss on stage. The other tough lesson omitted by *All About Eve* is that for every star there are thousands of women who lead washed-up, disappointed lives. Some of them wanted to act, but now their only pretence is that they contended. *All About Eve* never looks the audience in the eye and identifies us as the fickle bastards we are, greedy for a new look and so quickly bored.

Eve was a triumph – yet not a smash hit. It had cost about $1.25 milion and its domestic rentals were $2.9 million. That was good business, but it left the film way behind *Samson and Delilah* (rentals of $11 million). There was another lesson: the audience for great talk and not much action was real, but modest. Against that, *Eve* was nominated for fourteen Oscars (a record then) and won six – including best picture, best direction, best screenplay and best supporting actor (George Sanders).

The contest for best actress may have been the most distinguished ever: Gloria Swanson in *Sunset Boulevard*; Eleanor Parker in *Caged*; Judy Holliday in *Born Yesterday*; plus Bette Davis and Anne Baxter in *All About Eve*. Holliday won, and some have argued that that was only because Anne Baxter elected to contend as actress and not supporting actress. Of course, if the film is all about Eve then Eve feels central. But she's not on screen as much as Margo. And if Baxter had settled for supporting status then all she had to beat was Josephine Hull in *Harvey*, Hope Emerson in *Caged*, Nancy Olson in *Sunset Boulevard* or Celeste Holm or Thelma Ritter in *Eve*.

It doesn't much matter any more: Judy Holliday was revelatory and she was the new thing. As it was, Davis's nomination was her eighth (Katharine Hepburn, as yet, had only four). But here's another point: *All About Eve* still plays widely, yet Bette Davis had no residuals on the picture. She earned a higher weekly salary than ever before, with everything upfront. But 1950 was also the year in which James Stewart (using Bette's agent, Lew Wasserman) earned 50 per cent of the gross on a picture called *Winchester 73*. A man's deal.

For Bette it was a comeback and a magnificent setting for her rather hunted glamour. Margo is so vivid and large a character, and so adroitly linked with an attractive middle-aged man, that there is no romantic strain in the set-up. Indeed, it felt so natural, that Davis and Merrill promptly fell in love. There's something 'perfect' yet gruesome in that move. They were married and it would prove the longest marriage of her life. They adopted two children, a girl and a boy, as company for B.D., and they worked together a few more times, in *Another Man's Poison* and *Phone Call from a Stranger*. But she had a vision, of family life in Maine, that was simply at odds with the schedule of anyone who worked as much as she did.

Bette Davis seemed to be a big star still – she made *The Star*, *The Virgin Queen* (as Elizabeth Regina again), *Storm Center* and *The Catered Affair*. But no one believed she could carry a picture any longer and no one was happy with the way she looked. The very uneasy concept in *The Star* – that Bette was playing a real movie star who recognized the need to retire – was far from Bette Davis's opinion of herself. Perhaps she thought it was a picture about Joan Crawford. But she was in demand; in 1954, it was Bette who handed his Oscar to Marlon Brando – a big moment at the Oscars evening.

Here I was, back in the swing again. This time, not with as much enthusiasm. My real happiness was at home with the children. I felt this was where a mother ought to be. I didn't want to uproot them and move back to California. For the next few years Gary and I struggled to keep our home and somehow to keep each other. Although I closed my ears to the fact it was all too apparent that it was a losing battle. When *All About Eve* was finished, Gary and I had asked Mankiewicz to write a sequel. Now we were writing it for him – and no happy ending was in sight.

In hindsight, *The Star* was an uneasy, slight picture. Margaret Elliot is a star with an Oscar. People still recognize her. She could be forty-four – Bette's age – and she is broke. In the movie's first scene she is in the back of the room at an auction sale of her possessions, intimidated by a huge star picture of herself. She is out of work. She has her daughter (Natalie Wood) just six months a year. She meets a former co-star (Sterling Hayden), a guy who has given up acting for sailing. She tries to make a return, but she makes a fool of herself by asking for a 'younger' part. And so she retires.

Stuart Heisler directed, and the script was by Katherine Albert and Dale Euson. It lacks depth and feeling, and it's a marvel in hindsight that Davis got an Oscar nomination for it. Another nod that year went to Joan Crawford in *Sudden Fear*, a far more effective film, but the winner was Shirley Booth in *Come Back, Little Sheba*. What those nominations made clear was the need for younger female blood and skin on screen – and it would be supplied by Audrey Hepburn, Grace Kelly, Elizabeth Taylor, Marilyn Monroe, Ava Gardner, Leslie Caron and Deborah Kerr. It may be hard for older actresses, but anyone at the movies knows that the light feeds on youth.

The reprising of Queen Elizabeth was in a film where Richard Todd and Joan Collins were the romantic leads. *Storm Center* was a directorial debut for Daniel Taradash – the screenwriter on *From Here to Eternity* – and it was a worthwhile project. Alicia Hull (Davis) is a small-town librarian, a radical when younger, who resists pressure and keeps a Communist book on the shelves. She comes under increasing attack, and then a boy who adores her sets fire to the library. It's a picture with its heart in the right place, and Davis copes ably as an opinionated woman under attack. But the central relationship with the boy does not work very well, and the film seems very flat nowadays.

That is the very opposite of *The Catered Affair*, an unexpected slice of working-class comedy and a smooth amalgam of the talents of Paddy Chayefsky (original playwright) and Gore Vidal (credited screenwriter). It's a family story, but this is the family: Ernest Borgnine and Bette Davis are married, and Debbie Reynolds is their daughter – resist that if you can! Debbie wants to marry Rod Taylor and all the fuss is over the scale of the wedding and the aspirations of people who have very little money. What frees the film at the outset, is the enormous, gulp-like emotional shift Borgnine and Davis have to make to believe they are married. They are successful and the film is funnier than anyone might anticipate. Richard Brooks directed with high energy and Davis seems invigorated by the complete abandon-ment of any idea of looking chic or pretty. It is one of the few occasions on which Bette Davis had an authen-tic character part.

The marriage to Gary Merrill broke down in 1957, no matter that they toured *The World of Carl Sandburg* together in the theatre in the hope of building bonds. A few years earlier, Bette had also tried the stage in a review, *Two's Company*. She was to get $3,000 a week and 10 per cent of the box office, but the show foun-dered, and lost money. Indeed, throughout the '50s, there is the startling revelation that Bette Davis was actually hard up. The greatest star of her age, and the hardest-working, with a shelf of movies that were beginning to enjoy an extra life through television, still she was short of funds. It was in an effort to make money that she agreed to play Maxine Faulk in Tennessee Williams' play, *The Night of the Iguana*, in 1961. This was not ideal casting (Ava Gardner would get the part in the film), and Davis suffered in the reviews in comparison with her co-star, Margaret Leighton. In addition, she fought so much with director Frank Corsaro that she eventually had him banned from the house. But Davis was such an attraction that every night on her entrance the show stopped for an ovation. The rest of the cast were offended by this melodrama, but Bette milked the applause for all she was worth. Not too long into the run, she was replaced by Shelley Winters.

Again, she was miscast when Frank Capra hired her to play Apple Annie in *Pocketful of Miracles*, but the actress could not resist the fee of $100,000. Historically, the movies were beset by inflation: Elizabeth Taylor would be paid $1 million for *Cleopatra*, and here was Davis (in a supporting part) getting not much less than she had been paid for *All About Eve*, ten years ago. Equally, she was only fifty-four, and she had three children to support, not to mention her mother and her sister. The mother died in 1961, during the making of *Pocketful of Miracles*. The sister, Bobbie, continued to suffer from nervous breakdowns and was always in need of care. So the scene was set for the final onslaught upon the dignity of Bette Davis.

It was in 1962 that Bette Davis published her autobiography so far, *The Lonely Life*. It was not a self-pitying book. Indeed, many reviewers esteemed it for its candour, its clear writing and its steady gaze. Near the end

of that book, Davis wrote about the final explosion
between her and Gary Merrill: it was on the road with
Carl Sandburg in San Francisco, the city where much
of *All About Eve* had been filmed: 'I am sure I have
been uncompromising, peppery, untractable, monoma-
niacal, tactless, volatile and oft-times disagreeable. I
stand accused of it all. But at forty I allowed the female
to take over. It was too late. I admit that Gary broke my
heart. He killed the dream forever. The little woman no
longer exists.'

Movie stars were not what they had been. Around
1960, many great stars died (and rather younger than
the average age in America): Bogart, Gable, Gary
Cooper, after a decade in which those stalwarts had
been asked to play opposite women young enough to
be their daughters. It was in the '60s, that repertory
movie theatres and television late shows would redis-
cover the 'old' movie and the history of the stars. But in
the real world, film stars were being edged aside by TV
celebrities, by great sports heroes and even by poli-
ticians who looked like movie stars. All of this was
natural, a part of changing times. But there was another
thing in the air – vultures of scorn or derision, ready to
feed off the dying stars. The great figures of the past
began to be mocked. In a way the movies had started
that themselves with *Sunset Boulevard*. And films like *The
Star*. Then there was *Psycho* – one of the most influential
movies ever made, not just for its unrestrained violence
or cruelty, but because of the way a movie star – Janet

Leigh – was simply erased 40 minutes into a picture. There were film-makers itching to learn from *Psycho*'s drastic and satirical lack of respect.

One of those people was the director Robert Aldrich who had made some of the most striking American films of the '50s – a Western, about Indians, *Apache*, a scathing rebuke to the world of Mickey Spillane, *Kiss Me Deadly*, and an anti-war film, *Attack!* He had also done a picture called *Autumn Leaves* (1956), about a troubled romance between Joan Crawford and a younger man, Cliff Robertson. It was the kind of movie Bette Davis could have done if it had been possible to sustain belief in her sexual life on screen in 1956.

At this point, we have to say something about the Joan Crawford who seemed to haunt Davis's life. When Metro dumped Crawford in the mid-'40s, she was devastated. Her rally was all the braver and more determined – though some said that the icon of determination had made her face unbearably hard. She tottered on the brink of self-parody sometimes. She might be impossibly autocratic in person, and hell to work with. Still, in the years following *Mildred Pierce* she had done *Humoresque*, *Possessed*, *Flamingo Road*, *Harriet Craig*, *Sudden Fear*, *Johnny Guitar* and *Autumn Leaves*.

Moreover, Warner Brothers had had the two wilful lives together if only to provoke the publicity about their feuding. And if the two women often played up the feud themselves, that was a mark of good humour and mutual dislike. They didn't get on: Joan felt Bette

With Gary Merrill

had a class edge on her, while Bette was hurt by Joan's love life. In fact, by the late '50s, in terms of marital history and their retinue of children, real or adopted, they were close to being sisters.

Crawford had liked Aldrich. He said she offered to sleep with him, but he'd always been too busy. Still, Crawford urged him – can't we do another picture together? It was in 1960 that Aldrich read Henry Farrell's novel, *What Ever Happened to Baby Jane?*, a grotesque account of the life of the Hudson sisters, Jane and Blanche – the one a child star, the other an adult star, both sisters in a kind of tortured old age where Jane looks after the crippled Blanche and dreams of a demented comeback. And Aldrich thought of it as material for Crawford and Davis. He bought the rights to the novel for $17,500 and hired Lukas Heller to write a script. He let Joan see the first draft and she said she was ready. She also visited Bette one night after *The Night of the Iguana*, showed her the script and said this was their chance, at long last, to be together.

Davis was intrigued, especially when told that she was wanted for the more active and spectacular role of Jane. Aldrich was having trouble raising the backing – there were some people who could only feel its thickly spread bad taste. So the deal worked out like this: Davis would get $60,000 up front plus 10 per cent of the net profits worldwide; Joan would get only $30,000 and 15 per cent of the profits. The women signed on, though Bette negotiated a potent expenses item for herself, which eventually had to be given to Joan, too. At the time, Crawford's status was clearly higher: her recent pictures had done better and though Alfred Steele, her fifth husband, had died in 1959, she had inherited his shares in and board position with Pepsi-Cola.

It added to nostalgia and the stink of exploitation that Aldrich hired Ernest Haller to shoot *What Ever Happened to Baby Jane?* He had photographed *Dangerous*, *Jezebel*, *Dark Victory* and *Mr Skeffington*, as well as *Mildred Pierce* and *Humoresque*. But Haller was now under instruction to forsake the romantic lighting of those films in favour of a garish, ravaged look, in which ill-applied make-up feels like scars or tears of grief on the elderly faces. The two actresses were in their early fifties, but they should have guessed that they would look worse than they had ever done before. And to the extent that Aldrich was borrowing clips from their past films, he was cannibalizing that hallowed imagery. The Hudson sisters – dead or alive – were headed for the asylum that looked after Norma Desmond.

All the energy is Bette's. She runs the house in her scatterbrained way. She serves her sister with grilled rat. She fusses over the details of her comeback. She does the hideously violent things. And at the end, it is Bette who has the heartbreaking scene on the beach where Baby Jane slips back into her past.

The picture was a lurid success (it was released ironically by Warner Brothers, though they had declined to fund it). Bette Davis was nominated as best actress

What Ever Happened to Baby Jane?

(her tenth). Joan Crawford was overlooked. And there was a supporting actor nod to Victor Buono as the fat, creepy fan to Baby Jane. The film had a domestic box office over $4 million and a worldwide figure of $9 million. It looked at least as if the two actresses had sold themselves away for a fair price. The film cost under $1 million, and the claim went out that it recovered those costs in eleven days.

Then something happened, as it can in Hollywood where accounting is one of the arts and sciences. On the figures quoted already, *Baby Jane* should have been at least $5 million in profit. So Bette could have expected $500,000, enough to guard against old age. In the event, her profits bonus was only about 10 per cent of that sum. As for the Oscar, it went to Anne Bancroft in *The Miracle Worker*. More notably, one of the other contenders that year was Katharine Hepburn in *Long Day's Journey Into Night* – a very impressive example of what an actress could do past the age of fifty, and a happy indication of what the 'senior' Hepburn would manage.

By contrast, after *Baby Jane*, in the years from 1964 to 1988, Bette Davis delivers another twenty-eight films for theatre and television. Joan Crawford died in 1977 but she made only five more. Katharine Hepburn, on the other hand, earned three more Oscars as an 'elderly' person, in *Guess Who's Coming to Dinner?*, *The Lion in Winter* and *On Golden Pond*. Hers is the greatest achievement in longevity and in making a pensionable status seem desirable.

Bette Davis died in Paris, aged eighty-one, on 6 October 1989. I do not propose to go through the more than two decades that followed *Baby Jane* in detail – though it is plain to anyone that Davis stood up under financial difficulty, stroke and then cancer and never gave up fighting. In 1989, she was given a life achievement award by the Film Society of Lincoln Center. She attended the event in a wheelchair, but at the key moment she walked to the microphone, surveyed the assembly, and said, 'What a dump!' It was a crowd-pleasing line, full of spunk, yet it was also a concession to camp.

The later films? Well, there is *Dead Ringer*, directed by her old friend Paul Henreid. There is *Hush . . . Hush Sweet Charlotte*, a reunion with Aldrich and Henry Farrell, and a picture that couldn't persuade Joan Crawford to try it again. There is *The Nanny*, a pretty good horror suspense film made in England and directed by Seth Holt. There is her cameo in *Death on the Nile*. There was even, in 1987, *The Whales of August*, made with Ann Sothern and Lillian Gish, where Davis apparently scared the ever-sweet Gish close to death. I have not examined these later films. I chose to use my space by dwelling on the many fascinating pictures Bette made in her heyday, when nearly every film seemed to add to the dream-life of women.

She saw the death of Joan Crawford, and must have read *Mommie Dearest* – the book by Joan's adopted

daughter, Christina – with mixed feelings. But she
was heard to lament the shocking book and the horror of having a child turn on you. Still, it happened to
her, too: in 1985, B. D. Hyman published a book, *My
Mother's Keeper*, on how tough it had been being Bette's
daughter.

Well, yes, being a daughter is tough along with being
a mother and being alive. There is also being an actress,
and trying to compete with your mother's characters.

In her last years, Bette Davis was unrecognizable in
all except her voice. That stayed strong and demanding.
She also lived long enough to hear the Kim Carnes
song, 'Bette Davis Eyes'. The lyrics to that song were
not very interesting. But the fact of the song was proof
of an acknowledgement – central to this series of
books – that in the twentieth century we lived through
an age of immense romantic personalities larger than
life, yet models for it, too – for good or ill. Like twin
moons, promising a struggle and an embrace, the Davis
eyes would survive her – and us. Kim Carnes has hardly
had a consistent career, but that one song – sluggish yet
surging, druggy and dreamy – became an instant classic.
It's like the sigh of the islanders when they behold their
Kong. And I suspect it made the real eyes smile, whatever else was on their mind.

A Note on Sources

The valuable book, with Bette's authentic voice, is *The Lonely Life* (New York, 1962). Bette Davis wrote that book. Decades later, with Michael Herskowitz, she published *This 'n' That* (New York, 1987), which is less reliable or useful and which comes after B. D. Hyman's *My Mother's Keeper* (New York, 1985). There is also Charles Higham's *Bette: The Life of Bette Davis* (New York, 1981), Whitney Stine's *Mother Goddamn* (New York, 1974) and Charlotte Chandler's *The Girl Who Walked Home Alone: Bette Davis, a Personal Biography* (New York, 2006), which is novelistic. But don't miss Sam Staggs' *All About 'All About Eve'* (New York, 2000).

Filmography

1935   *Bordertown*
      The Girl from 10th Avenue
      Front Page Woman
      Special Agent
      Dangerous (Oscar win for Best Actress in a
          Leading Role)

1936   *The Petrified Forest*
      The Golden Arrow
      Satan Met a Lady

1937   *Marked Woman*
      Kid Galahad
      That Certain Woman
      It's Love I'm After

1938   *Jezebel* (Oscar win for Best Actress in a Leading
          Role)
      The Sisters

1939   *Dark Victory* (Oscar nomination for Best
          Actress in a Leading Role)
      Juarez
      The Old Maid
      The Private Lives of Elizabeth and Essex

1940   *If I Forget You*
      All This, and Heaven Too
      The Letter (Oscar nomination for Best Actress
          in a Leading Role)

1941   *The Great Lie*
      Shining Victory (uncredited cameo role)
      The Bride Came C.O.D.

The Little Foxes (Oscar nomination for Best
　　Actress in a Leading Role)

1942　*The Man Who Came to Dinner*
　　In This Our Life
　　Now, Voyager (Oscar nomination for Best
　　Actress in a Leading Role)

1943　*Watch on the Rhine*
　　Old Acquaintance

1944　*Mr Skeffington* (Oscar nomination for Best
　　Actress in a Leading Role)

1945　*The Corn Is Green*

1946　*A Stolen Life*
　　Deception

1948　*Winter Meeting*
　　June Bride

1949　*Beyond the Forest* ·

1950　*All About Eve* (Oscar nomination for Best
　　Actress in a Leading Role)

1951　*Payment on Demand*

1952　*Another Man's Poison*
　　Phone Call from a Stranger
　　The Star (Oscar nomination for Best Actress in
　　a Leading Role)

1955　*The Virgin Queen*

1956　*The Catered Affair*
　　Storm Center

1959　*John Paul Jones*
　　The Scapegoat

1961   *Pocketful of Miracles*

1962   *What Ever Happened to Baby Jane?* (Oscar
            nomination for Best Actress in a Leading
            Role)

1963   *The Empty Canvas*

1964   *Dead Ringer*
            Where Love Has Gone
            Hush . . . Hush, Sweet Charlotte

1965   *The Nanny*

1968   *The Anniversary*

1970   *Connecting Rooms*

1971   *Bunny O'Hare*

1972   *The Scientific Cardplayer*

1976   *Burnt Offerings*

1978   *Return from Witch Mountain*
            Death on the Nile
            The Children of Sanchez

1980   *The Watcher in the Woods*

1987   *The Whales of August*

1989   *Wicked Stepmother*

Picture Credits